# DATA-DRIVEN MARKETING

Lucy!

I love, love, love having you'm this team. If you're reading this and seeing me at the same time, it's obvious that we didn't win the lottery and the $5m I planned to give you will have to wait until the next "Big One"! Thank you for your ever present smile, collaborative spirit, and wry sense of humor. You're also known as the "GBP/Ecosystem autocorrector" LOL. I appreciate your significant and amazing contributions to our team!

Jacqueline

# DATA-DRIVEN MARKETING

Leverage data to increase sales, grow profits, and land more customers

Roger Bryan

**Ainsley&Allen**
PUBLISHING

Data-Driven Marketing – Third Edition 4 3 2 1 0
ISBN-13: 978-1-946694-02-7
ISBN-10: 1-946694-02-9

Library of Congress Control Number: 2017938468

As this book goes to the publisher I have a term
sheet on my desk to sell my third digital business.

I often get asked, "What is the secret to my
ability to start, scale, and sell digital businesses?"

The Answer: DATA

For all the nights spent on the road researching this book, and for all the crazy ideas you support, this book is dedicated to my amazing wife, Krista.

To show my appreciation to you the reader I've also provided a great deal on our AI Powered Local Marketing Software: Enfusen

If you like what you read in this book head on over to https://www.enfusen.com and sign up for a trial. You can use the code "DataDriven50" to receive a LIFETIME Discount of 50% off any subscription.

Thanks for buying my book!

# CONTENTS

# PREFACE

## What You Will Learn From This Book

This book will outline everything you need as a marketer to systematically implement data-driven marketing in your organization. I've chosen to follow the *Five Phases of Data Driven Marketing* as laid out by CMO.com. The five phases include: Gather, Understand, Decide and Automate, Execute, Test and Learn. I find that following this path will help you to implement a successful strategy the very first time.

I spent three years working with hundreds of businesses on their "Modern Marketing Strategies." I found that the most successful businesses all had one thing in common: an understanding of how to leverage data in their marketing efforts.

It doesn't matter if you're a marketing agency owner, a CMO, or a college student looking for your first marketing internship, by the end of this book, you will be armed with an understanding of how data can make your life easier, and how data-driven marketing can make your campaigns more successful.

# The True Stages of Data-Driven Marketing
## (joking... well... a little)

© marketoonist.com

# INTRODUCTION

After 20 years as a professional marketer, I've seen plenty of trends. I've watched companies like AOL go from industry leaders to forgotten relics of the past. I've watched early entry companies like MySpace fall to the current titan of social media, Facebook. I have no idea what the next big company will be. The one thing I do know is that any company today that wants to be around in five years needs to have a critical understanding of one thing: Data.

I never set out to be a marketer. My career started out as an electrical engineer as an active duty Marine. When I finished my tour, I expected to get a job with one of the major defense contractors or airlines. The universe, as it often does, had different plans for me.

When I left the military, I decided to get a business degree. This meant I was also going to have to get a job. I ended up taking an inventory management job at an auto auction in Cleveland, OH. I could say this is where my marketing experience began, but that would be overlooking the way many marketers cut their teeth.

It was 1997 and I was stationed at Camp Pendleton, CA. I had just been assigned my barracks and purchased my first modern computer. (I had a Commodore 64 as a kid. Who else remembers using tapes to save their programming?) The Internet was still new to me, as it was to most. I became obsessed with chat rooms, online photo galleries, and email. Wow, was I amazed by email. As with any new thing, the opportunities to earn money online were limitless. I just needed to find my place.

My first attempt at this was a website reseller program. I would go into chat rooms and talk to business owners about the power of a website. I had no idea what I was doing, but I knew I would get half of the $497 they would have to pay to get a one page website with a domain. I worked for weeks learning how to pitch websites to strangers. In the end, I sold one, and then moved on.

Then came Excel Phone Services. Yes, I tried a network marketing long distance phone service that gave customers a FREE pager when they signed up for long distance service.

My hook with this was selling 1-800#'s to guys in the barracks who could then call home at a lower rate than what the phone company on base charged us. It was about 1/5th the cost. I remember selling to 52 people my first month. Within a few months, I was making more money selling phone services than I was getting paid by Uncle Sam.

The desire to hustle was always there. I didn't know where it came from and I didn't know where it was going to lead me. I just kept moving.

Each time, I found myself a victim of external circumstances. Web design became more common and better offers came to market. The phone company I was working for went bankrupt. My time in the military came to an end, and with that so did my captive audience to sell things to. We won't talk about the tax return company I started online in 1999. That one got me in a bit of trouble with the IRS.

The point is everyone comes from different backgrounds. We all have different skills and experience. Whatever your background is, my goal is that this book helps you to do one of three things:

1. Grow your business through the use of data-driven marketing
2. Help you bring a product to market through the use of data-driven marketing
3. Help you to grow your Digital Marketing Agency through the use of data-driven marketing

Let's get started.

# What is the Focus of This Book?

We each have our super power. Mine has been the ability to start, scale, and sell digital businesses. I saw with this book an opportunity to both layout the foundation for data-driven marketing that can be used by everyone, while also adding tips and advice on how digital business owners can leverage these skills to service their organizations.

The strategies in this book have been used in all kinds of industries: nonprofit, healthcare, IT, software, automotive, and local services, to name a few.

There is something in this book for every marketer.

The strategies behind data-driven marketing are always changing. I'd love to learn more about the projects you're working on and what you may have discovered.

Let's connect on Facebook to discuss the world of Data-Driven Marketing.

Facebook.com/MarketingWithRoger

– Roger Bryan

# Why You Need to Embrace a Data-Driven Marketing Strategy

While teaching at a local university last week, I asked my students this question: "How many people here are marketing students?"

Every hand in the class flew up into the air, which was no surprise; I was teaching a marketing class.

I then asked, "How many of you are analytics or data science students?" Not a single hand went up. I then broke the news, "I'm sorry, five years from now, you will all be out of work."

Long story short: Without adopting a data-driven method, you're going to be out of a job in five years. The future is data-driven.

The modern marketer cannot survive without data-driven marketing.

## There's no way around that fact.

What do I mean by this? Marketing as we know it is dying. There will be less and less need for marketing professionals in the future. The everyday marketer that makes social media posts, writes blog posts, and puts together email funnels will be, and is already being, replaced by machines.

In the future, there will be two types of 'marketers.'

The first will be the creative types. Those masters of words and images that can craft a message that brings a brand to life.

If you are one of those creative types (I'm not), you can relax. Well, at least for a few more years. The machines are coming after your jobs as well.

The other will be the data analyst. The scientist that can work with the machines to logically examine industry data and trends to develop products specifically designed to fill a known need. They will have the skill and understanding to leverage data to bring their product to market and to put one in every home.

If you're not a wicked copywriter or a top-notch graphic designer, which I'm not, then you better learn to make data your best friend. Let me see if I can help you with that.

# SECTION 1:
# GETTING STARTED

# What is Data-Driven Marketing?

Data-driven marketing refers to marketing insights and decisions that arise from the analysis of data about, or from, consumers. The goal of data-driven marketing is to build a better relationship with your current and potential customers by understanding how they interact with your organization's marketing message.

## The Data-Driven Methodology

Data-driven marketing can also be referred to as database marketing, or the use of customer data, customer contact and engagement, as well as the analytics that combine to create predictable and dependable outcomes from marketing campaigns. Simply put, data-driven marketing is the act of leveraging data to increase the output of marketing campaigns. Almost every single person reading this book is already using data-driven marketing in one way or another. If you've created a persona from Facebook demographics or if you've tried email marketing throughout your organization, you are using data-driven marketing. Don't worry if you haven't done any of this before. This book will guide you through the process.

## 5 Major Benefits of Data-Driven Marketing

### 1. Targeting

Let's start with the ability to deliver the right message to the right person at exactly the right time.

The sales professional that offers a solution to a known problem is rarely turned away. Why? Because consumers are always looking for solutions to their problems.

Anyone that's in inbound, digital, or data-driven marketing has heard that a lot. You mostly hear it from the big players like the Salesforce Cloud, the Adobe Cloud, and the Oracle Cloud. These are people that are using predictive analytics in order to analyze what you're doing and who you're trying to connect with so that you can deliver the exact right message to the exact right person at the exact right time.

Throughout this book, I'm going to show you how can get the same results in your organization without having to pay a quarter of a million dollars a year to have access to the data and tools that you need to make it happen.

## 2. Forecast Opportunities

Believe it or not, there are many companies and organizations that invest in data-sustained marketing to improve their internal operations.

From optimizing and making predictions on inventory, to collecting data that helps your team determine seasonal demands, the technology needed to create a solid digital marketing strategy empowers the whole of your business.

As the marketing machine collects the data you need to reach your ideal customers, it also records the activity that is currently taking place in your business to help employees and managers alike maintain healthy systems of operations.

## 3. Reduce Financial Risk

No matter how you slice it, your online dollars can take your business a long way if you're spending in the right places. This is really about content delivery that matches where your customer is in the buying cycle.

The financial risk with the implementation of any marketing campaign is whether or not it's going to work. If it doesn't, you're out the time, energy and resources that a failed campaign doesn't deliver on. If you use data, the probability of success increases exponentially which therefore decreases the risk associated with the implementation and the investment in the campaign.

With data intelligence and recommendation engines, your sales and marketing teams can focus on creating content that your customers will actually engage with. Better yet, there's always the potential for an outstanding piece of content to take off and become a hit. It's times like that where companies experience an influx of sales, potential customers, and newly interested consumers.

## 4. Increase Revenue

It's no secret that there's a lot of potential to make money in digital marketing. Unfortunately, modern marketers rarely feel that they're seizing all of that potential. With a data-based strategy, your team can take advantage of that seemingly mythical potential. Not only will you be able to provide content and offers that entice first-time visitors into customers, you'll be receiving the data you need from those interactions to determine where you need to improve.

As you grow and develop, you'll be using data inside your own organization to grow sales momentum and apply that same data for the same end result, no matter whom the client is. You'll grow and learn how to understand the wants and needs of the organization without pestering them with questions.

Your ability to increase revenue is based upon the data you have that justifies the proposal you make to a client. Learning how to leverage data helps you offer solutions to problems they may not know exist.

## 5. Dependable, Predictable Growth

Perhaps the very best benefit of employing data-driven solutions in your business is the potential created by a thriving return on investment. The more that can come from the money you spend on sales and marketing, the better. That's just a simple facet of business.

More importantly, it gives your sales and marketing departments the ability to work on growth.

Once you have the data and know what's working for your business as a whole, your team can work on furthering already successful marketing campaigns into larger revenue streams.

With the room to work on nurturing solid campaigns into rock star campaigns, your team can begin to drive new growth and revenue.

# CHAPTER 2

# The Research

The foundation of this book comes from the 24 months my team and I spent with our partner, Microsoft, as part of their Modern Marketer Program. The methodologies used in implementing data-driven marketing were derived from countless hours spent working one-on-one with B2B sellers inside their partner network.

During this time, we performed 438 initial discussions about modern marketing practices and marketing strategy. We did in-depth marketing assessments of 126 organizations that uncovered the primary problems most organizations were facing with marketing. We then took this knowledge and ran 45 marketing campaigns to leverage what we learned. These efforts have been documented for you in this book.

Working with these organizations, we discovered that the industry lacked a clear defined process for implementing data-driven marketing inside organizations of all sizes. Despite their efforts, many marketers still needed direction when it comes to leveraging data in their marketing efforts.

## The Problem Organizations are Facing

The first goal of our project was to uncover exactly what was stopping organizations from achieving marketing success. At the onset of this project, data was just one of 20 different elements we were examining. Here were some of our initial findings:

- Organizations lacked clearly-defined buyer personas
- The ability to identify opportunities in their organization's sales and marketing efforts
- Understanding the different channels at which marketing works best for their organization
- Having access to and knowing how to use the correct technology

A basic understanding of data can solve all of these issues.

## Results in Detail

Our participation in the program created five important lessons that became the foundation for our program and then for this book. Organizations that grasped these lessons had the greatest success implementing data-driven marketing campaigns.

## Lesson One: Ability to gather and organize sales and marketing data

78.2% of the organizations we worked with had three or more places they needed to go to find their sales and marketing data. This could be multiple CRM platforms, spreadsheets, piles of business cards, or even sticky notes on a white board. We found that the first thing we needed to do in every campaign was to combine all of their data into one platform. In data science, this is called "data wrangling." In data-driven marketing, it's called cleaning up an unorganized mess. Really, neither is that different.

## Lesson Two: An understanding of the primary data points in a campaign

In 96.2% of our campaigns, organizations lacked a clear understanding of what the most important data points were. This lack of understanding was a key element to why their campaigns had failed in the past. If you don't know what to track, then you can't track it.

How many of you reading this book feel like you don't know what it is that you don't know when it comes to data-driven marketing? If you have this feeling, you're not alone. You need to remember that we were talking to multi-million dollar companies who did not have a defined sales process, nor did they have an understanding of the supporting data needed to grow their organization.

## Lesson Three: Choosing the right technology for the campaign

We are all constantly being bombarded with new technology. There are well over 1000 different sales and marketing tools out there you can use today. It's very easy to get overwhelmed to the point of analysis paralysis or, even worse, to start buying every tool hoping one of them is a magic bullet.

No tool will solve all of your problems, but mastering one of the main CRM or Marketing Automation Tools can be key to your success.

## Lesson Four: Educating and empowering their staff

Of the 438 organizations we spoke with, only TWO had a formal training program for their sales and marketing staff. ONLY TWO! In almost every case, organizations attempted to hire staff to fill gaps in their marketing and sales teams. The right way to do this is to train the staff you have. The marketing skills of today are most certainly going to be obsolete in two years. In some cases with technology, this can happen even faster.

It is critical that you constantly be in a learning mode. You need to be training yourself and your staff no matter what type of business you're in.

## Lesson Five: Creating goal-based campaigns and then measuring the results of their efforts

It sounds simple. Set a goal. That's because it is simple. Yet, most marketers don't set goals in their campaigns. We have an entire chapter on setting marketing goals in this book. Please never launch a campaign without a predetermined goal or outcome. Without this target, how will you know if what you did was successful?

Before building your first data-driven marketing campaign, let's take a look at two program participants, the problems they faced, the solutions we designed, and the outcome of those efforts.

# Partner Case Study: CAL Business Solutions

**Business Solutions Provider...**
moving you forward.

## The Problem

CAL Business Solutions had sales and marketing automation in mind for quite some time, but lacked the focused plan that was needed to implement.

- Understanding the data they had
- Lacked a defined data-driven buyer persona
- Their data was spread out between multiple tools and spreadsheets
- Lacked the right technology to implement success campaigns
- Had an empowered staff, but needed training on modern marketing technology
- Did not have defined campaign goals

## The Solution

We educated their staff on data-driven principles that helped them define their buyer persona. Their extraordinary team was able to implement new technology and to gather and organize their data in less than 90 days.

## The Outcome

A 275% increase in Marketing Qualified Leads.

# Partner Case Study: Fifth Avenue Brands

## The Problem

Fifth Avenue Brands had an amazing product offer, but lacked a go-to-market strategy to scale.

- Lacked a defined data-driven buyer persona
- Lacked a targeted list of potential buyers
- Lacked the right technology to implement successful campaigns
- Had an empowered staff, but needed training on modern marketing technology
- Did not have defined campaign goals

## The Solution

We built a buyer persona around business owners who made the Inc. 5000, created a go-to-market strategy to leverage their accomplishment, and connected this with the Public Relation Services being offered.

## The Outcome

Doubled sales in six months.

# SECTION 2: GATHER

# CHAPTER 3

# Understanding Data

Let's start simple: *What is Data?*

The dictionary definition of data is:

> *Facts and statistics collected together for reference or analysis*

This is a very straightforward definition.

So the question becomes: What data is needed to run a data-driven marketing campaign? We'll answer that question in this chapter.

# The Data Points You Need to Know

Let's do a high-level overview of each of the main data points you'll need to know to implement you first data-driven campaign. I'm going to briefly mention some technology platforms that are used to capture, analyze, and manage these data points as well. Don't worry; I've dedicated an entire chapter to recommended technology platforms.

One note on this chapter: Don't get too bogged down with the details here. This is an introduction to these terms. We'll show you how to use these data points later in the book. This is not a complete list of every possible type of data. These are the most important elements needed to setup your campaign.

## Persona Data

Persona data are the data points that help you to define and isolate your ideal buyer.

## Lead Stage Data

Lead Stage Data is used to tell exactly where a prospect is in the buying process. This is not an absolute linear process, nor is the sales process over when someone buys. Having defined lead stages allows you to easily manage the sale and upsell conversation.

## Engagement Data

In between each sales stage, you'll be engaging with your prospects. It's important to define and capture specific points of engagement so you can continue to nurture your prospect towards the ideal outcome.

## Marketing Data

Marketing Data or 'Campaign Data' are the statistics generated from marketing campaigns. I've placed them after lead stages and engagement to outline a critical point. It's vital that you define all of your data points before you launch a single campaign. This will help you to maximize your returns.

### Campaign Key Performance Indicators (KPIs)

These are your macro Key Performance Indicators. This is typically a small set of data points that let you know at an executive level if your campaign was a success.

Let's break these down into their smallest parts.

## Persona Data

If you've ever purchased a list, you may have been sent well over 70 different columns in the report. There is a ton of great data out there that you can acquire about your prospects. We are going to outline the five critical pieces of data you need in order to know if your prospect fits your ideal avatar.

I often get asked about budget, authority, need, and timing (BANT) at this point. While those are important elements in proper targeting, we're going to start from a high-level perspective and work our way down. The following data points are all stats that you can buy from numerous different list brokers or data providers. You can also find a lot of this data via publicly available websites if you want to do it by hand.

The seller that tries to sell to everyone typically sells no one. Define whom you're trying to sell to and you'll have a lot more success.

I've also outlined the persona elements of my business, Enfusen. This will give you a first hand look at how we apply these exact same rules in our every day operations.

## Annual Revenue

What is the annual revenue of your ideal buyer? A company that does $500,000 in sales is going to have different wants and needs than a company that does $100,000,000 per year. In most cases, your product isn't going to be for companies of all sizes.

*Enfusen's Persona: Annual Revenue*
*We target agencies in the $500,000 to $10,000,000 for our analytics platform. Agencies under $500,000 really are not ready for the powerful tools we provide. Agencies that do over $10,000,000 can usually afford the enterprise version of tools like ours. I'll cover some of these tools later in the book. Some of them can run upwards of $250,000 per year for a single site where Enfusen starts at $6,000 per year for multiple sites.*

## Employee Size

Knowing the size of your ideal buyer's team is critical to defining your sales process. The larger the organization, the more layers of people you will have to go through to get the approval you need to complete your sale.

*Enfusen's Persona: Employee Size*
*We target agencies with 5-49 employees. In many cases, the majority of the employees are part-time contractors or outsource workers. We've chosen this target as agencies*

*that are run by solopreneurs usually are not ready to work with us, while companies with over 50 employees fall again into the enterprise space and are using different tool sets.*

## Job Title

Who specifically inside the company are you trying to sell to? Is it the owner, the marketing director, someone in HR, or someone in facility management? Knowing the role of your buyer allows you to craft a message that resonates while also helping to define exactly what you'll need to do to reach them.

*Enfusen's Persona: Job Title*
*Greater than 90% of the time, we'll deal directly with the owner of the agency. There are cases with some of the larger agencies we work with where someone in the C-Suite like the CMO may have run into us at an event and brought us to the owner. This again goes with the size of the agencies we work with.*

## Industry

You must have a primary industry that you serve. This is even more important when you're first starting out. I've worked in a few different industries in my career: Nonprofits, Microsoft Partners, and Marketing Agencies. Each has their own unique set of needs and problems. The more defined your persona is, the easier it is to target the right message to the right person.

*Enfusen's Persona: Industry*
*When we first started building the Enfusen Platform, it was actually designed for Microsoft Partners. It was an*

*advanced analytics platform using Business Intelligence (BI) to predict which marketing strategies would help partners go to market quickly and efficiently with new offers from Microsoft.*

*The problem was that most partners didn't have the team in place to leverage the data we provided. We had to make a choice. When we pivoted our business and decided to only work directly with marketing agencies, that is when everything changed for us. This simple (yet stressful at the time) decision helped us to triple our business in less than 90 days. The point here is to find a focus, but also stay flexible.*

## Geo Location

Defining the area you will serve is the important fifth element of a buyer persona. Are you going to target a specific city, a specific state, or a country? While deciding what your geo target will be, I always recommend to start local, but think global. If you can dominate your local market, you can dominate others.

*Enfusen's Persona: Geo Location*
*When we first launched our platform, it was targeted only at the US. We then expanded to Canada, the UK, Australia, and South Africa – all English-speaking countries where we were able to establish partnerships. As this book is being published we're finishing our next expansion round from 12 countries to 64. I like to practice what I preach. Start local, but think global.*

## Lead Stage Data

I've seen people use all kinds of different lead stages over the years. Some organizations have a simple three-bucket setup, while some enterprise organizations have upwards of 100. I've gone somewhat down the middle (don't worry; that doesn't mean 50). The clients that we've seen have success have used these ten lead stages in their business to properly account for where each prospect is in their funnel.

I will note that these funnels are designed to capture and track leads from all incoming sources to include data-mining, list acquisition, lead gen efforts, events, or any other source you can think of. If you haven't done a lot of list acquisition in the past, the first few stages may seem redundant. Stay with me and I'll make sense of all this.

Before we get into this, I want to define what a 'lead' is. This term is used too often for the wrong reason. Just because someone is a lead doesn't mean they are qualified or that they are a potential buyer. There is no lead stage 'lead.' There are different stages at which a lead goes through to qualify themselves. We will use the term 'lead' as any contact that is in our funnel going through our lead stages.

### Contact

A contact is anyone on your list that has not been qualified either due to not having the needed data, or having the correct data points, but not aligning with your persona. We place 'leads' in this bucket to signify that there is a data need before any sales or marketing efforts are applied to the lead.

*Example: You have a name, address, phone number, and email address from someone you met at an event. They were really nice and seemed very interested in what you do. Their business card unfortunately doesn't have their job title and you have no idea how big the company is.*

*Your first instinct is probably to set up a sales call and start working them towards that close. But is that the best way to ensure a deal gets done?*

*Take the information you have and then go to work to define the five primary data points from the persona section first. Leverage tools like LinkedIn Sales Navigator to figure out if this person is actually a potential buyer.*

## Prospect

A prospect is a lead that matches all five of your persona elements. This is a critical definition that can save you an amazing amount of time and money. The second biggest waste in any funnel (after poor ad spend) is the time spent working on leads that were never qualified. You can eliminate that by keeping leads in the contact bucket until they have persona match. You can then move them to the prospect list.

The prospect list is where your marketing begins. Now that they are qualified from a data perspective, it is time to engage them. As leads will come from different sources, the next step can have a couple of different paths. We'll get more into those when we talk about implementing your campaigns.

## Marketing Qualified Lead (MQL)

A Marketing Qualified Lead (MQL) is a prospect that has been engaged. Engagement means they have responded in some way to a marketing message that shows some level of interest in your offer. This can be a response to an email, the completion of a long form on your site, or attendance to a paid event. This doesn't necessarily show they are ready to buy. It just shows that they are engaged.

This is an important stage. This is the point where the marketing team is now ready to turn the lead over to sales. If the marketing team can qualify and engage a lead to this point of interest, the next step is to turn them into a Sales Qualified Lead.

**Sales Qualified Lead (SQL)**

A Sales Qualified Lead (SQL) is an MQL that has completed an initial discovery call and that has also expressed interest in continuing the sales conversation. The important elements here are:

- The are a persona match prospect
- They engaged with your offer (became an MQL)
- They have voluntarily completed a discovery process and are now waiting on a proposal

Some sales reps like to get trigger-happy here and move MQL's to SQL's when they schedule their sales conversation. That's a bit too early. You need to complete the sales conversation to a point where both parties are interested in moving to the proposal process.

**Opportunity**

We're now one step away from ringing that bell. A lead moves to the Opportunity stage the moment they acknowledge receipt of your proposal. You've completed the qualification, engagement, and discovery. Now all that is left for you to do is close the deal. Keeping this lead stage up to date is easy because it's where the majority of your future revenue is sitting.

**Won**

This one is pretty straightforward. When you sign the contract and deposit their check, you can mark the lead as won. This is the 'ring the bell' moment that we all work towards. This doesn't mean the sales process is over, but for the sake of this discussion it is the critical point of success.

**Loss**

You win some, you lose some. In fact, we all lose a lot (if you're trying that is). This lead stage is for deals that didn't close. Now that doesn't mean this is a dead lead. It just means you didn't win this round. We'll leave the lead here until we can trigger an activity to move it back out again.

**Do Not Contact**

From time to time we run into that pain in the ass that ever so politely tells you to get lost. This stage is reserved for those people that have made it super clear that they don't want anything to do with you AND you agree that it's not worth your time to pursue them. This stage should be used as little as possible. This is where leads go to die.

**Cold Lead**

We typically reserve this stage for a lead that has gone 180 days without a response to at least ten attempts to contact.

These attempts have to include at least one of each of the following: Email, Social Media (like LinkedIn), and a phone call. A great way for a sales rep to lose their job in an organization we work with is for them to place a lead in the cold lead stage because they didn't respond to a handful of emails. Pick up the phone and make sure they are still out there.

**Future Follow up**

The larger the deal you're working, the more likely you are to run into annual budgets, current contracts, or cycles that are beyond your control. It is best to document those issues and move the lead over to the future follow up stage. You would also want to add a trigger to notify you as to when you should reach back out.

## Engagement Data

At each lead stage, you'll be engaging with your lead in an attempt to move them forward. It is important to document this engagement so you know exactly what has been done or not done to move the lead forward. These are some of the most important engagement points.

**Last Email Open**

When was the last time your lead opened one of your emails? While not a powerful success factor data point, it at least lets us know they are still out there and that our email address is good. Make sure you're capturing this date.

**Last Site Visit (page/date)**

We need to know when our leads visit our website. We'll talk about tools that help you to do this in the technology chapter. Tracking what pages someone visits gives you the ammunition you need to close a deal.

*Example: Lead 'Bob Smith' visits your Pricing page > then your About Us page > then your Contact page > but he doesn't contact you. These are what we call 'trigger pages' meaning that you should have a trigger alert set up anytime one of your leads visits these critical pages. This is a sure sign that someone is thinking about buying but something stopped them from reaching out. Having the ability to track page visits will help you to know the exact right time to call or email a lead.*

**Last Connected Call**

In an email-obsessed world, the phone is a crucial missing piece in many campaigns. To properly execute data-driven campaigns, you need to make sure your sales team is tracking all of their phone calls in your CRM (more about that in the technology section). When it's time to craft your campaign, you'll define different strategies for leads that are at different points of the sales cycle. If you haven't reached out via phone to someone in your Opportunity stage in a while, it might be a good idea to start dialing.

**Lead Score**

Lead Scoring is an advanced metric that helps a professional sales team to leverage multiple data points inside a single metric.

This is a very powerful strategy to help target ideal buyers buried in your data.

*Example: When working with a large non-profit organization, one of the stages of our intake process is to setup lead scoring inside their CRM. Once we set this up and launched our first monthly newsletter, we had 11 leads that triggered our 'lead score is greater than 80' alert. When their major giving department looked at these leads, they instantly recognized nine of them, but two of the leads were not familiar to them.*

*With a little deeper of a dive, they found that one of the leads had given $1000 a year for the last three years, but had never been contacted by the major diving department. Within 30 days of this realization, the donor had stepped up to give an additional $30,000. Without lead scoring, the organization may have never realized this lead was floating around in their data.*

**Days in Stage**

This is an important metric that allows you to cleanse a stage by oldest lead in. It's important to keep your lead stages up to date. The easiest way to do this is to always start with the oldest leads first. Create an engagement strategy, reach out, and then define what to do with them next.

## Marketing Data

While I could write an entire book on different marketing metrics that you can consider, I'm going to stick to the most important ones that relate to a data-driven marketing campaign. If you can master these points, then you can scale just about any business.

## Cost per Impression

This is the cost per view of your ad. This is often measured as the cost per 1000 impressions just to keep the math easier.

## Cost per Engagement

This is the cost to get someone to engage with an ad or message. This used to be called cost per click (in some cases it still is, see below) but with the adoption of many social media ad strategies, it's now measured per engagement.

## Cost per Click

Running an ad with the sole intent to get someone to leave the ad and engage with an offer at another location.

## Click Through Rate

The percentage of people that click on your ad relative to the number of people that see the ad.

## Cost per Cookie

This is a figure calculated in remarketing campaigns. It's the cost per user that you've cookied to retarget with ads. This is another topic that could be an entire book on its own.

## Cost per Lead

This is the cost to put a lead in your database (CRM). This could be through marketing efforts, or it could be through list acquisition. It is important to know the cost of your lead so you can calculate the next data point.

## Cost per Acquisition

Cost per sale. It's the main data point every business owner should know. How much do you have to invest to get one new customer?

# Campaign KPI's

A KPI is a Key Performance Indicator. It can include many of the data points in the above section. In this book, it's only going to include three things: Campaign Spend, Campaign Revenue, and Campaign ROI.

## Campaign Spend

What is our total investment in this campaign? This should include all ad spend, technology spend, and labor costs.

## Campaign Revenue

What was the total revenue generated from this campaign? This isn't always something that is easy to calculate in the short term depending on your sales cycle. If you have a 30 days close, 90 days close, or in larger enterprise case, it could take years before a deal is expected to close.

## Campaign Return on Investment (ROI)

Campaign Return on Investment (ROI) is the campaign revenue divided by the campaign spend. We always hope for positive ROI campaigns but don't always get them. This book was written to help ensure high ROI.

CHAPTER 4

# The Right Data

There are a few macro campaign data points that you want to make sure to find before you go any further. These are the elements that are going to help craft your overall data-driven marketing campaign strategy.

# Setting the Stage for Success

## Your Budget

Later in this book, there is a chapter on goal setting, but for now part of your overall campaign strategy has to be a predefined budget for what you can spend implementing your campaign. Even if you're just reading along in this book to get a better understanding of data-driven marketing, it would be a good idea to write down on a piece of paper a potential budget for the implementation of a campaign. When you get to the chapters on different digital marketing channels and goal setting, you'll be able to better comprehend the information that's being shared if you can build it around this budget

## Defined Buyer Persona

At this point, you also need to have a buyer persona. We covered the five elements of a buyer persona in Section 2. These elements are company size, annual revenue, industry, job title, and geographical location.

This would be a good time for you to continue writing down some of the thoughts that you have about the campaign you want to create. If you haven't done so already, it would be a good idea to also write down your potential buyer persona. I always like to start a campaign design or strategy session around what we believe our ideal buyer is so that as we go through the data we can figure out if our assumptions are correct and if they are not, we can correct them.

## Defined Value Proposition

You will need a complete understanding of the value proposition that you're bringing to market. This would include the problem that you're solving, how you solve it, and the end result the client will see when their problem is solved.

The problem with many go-to-market strategies is they fail to define this value proposition in detail and then struggle to create content that supports their offer. Defining this now, even in a general sense, will allow you to continue through the book and update this data point so that at the end you will have a defined campaign strategy that allows you to go to market quickly and efficiently.

## Defined Offer

Once you've outlined your buyer persona and your value proposition, it's time to define your offer. We'll cover the overall sales funnel in a later chapter, but for now just write down your initial offer. This could be your trip wire offer, or it could be your final monetization offer, which is the goal of your entire campaign. This is whatever you're offering to the market to create a transaction.

## Defined Primary Marketing Channel

You should now choose your primary marketing channel as well. By defining this, you can start to look at your data from the perspective of how you're going to engage your ideal buyer. Start with one channel, define your strategy, and integrate that into your goal setting so that you at least have one metric that you can follow along with. In most data-driven marketing campaigns, you're going to leverage multiple digital marketing channels. Typical combinations could be SEM, content marketing, email marketing, and possibly an element of social selling. Not every campaign is the same, nor is every organization's ability to implement the channels.

## Notes for Agency Owners

If you are a digital agency owner, this is a good time to start to document your strengths from a digital channel perspective so that you know how to craft your offer to potential customers. What is your superpower when it comes to marketing? How can you leverage that to create successful data-driven marketing campaigns?

## Initial Pieces of Content

The last element for your data-driven marketing campaign is crafting some of your needed content. You want to break this into three parts:

1. **Awareness**: Content used to create awareness about your brand, your position, and your authority in the space.
2. **Consideration**: Content used to help guide potential buyers into your sales funnel based on your value proposition and your ability to solve their current pain.
3. **Decision**: Content that is used to directly engage a potential buyer with your offer. At this point, they need to be willing to give their contact information to you in exchange for some type of tangible value.

This is a very basic overview of how to put together the needed content for your campaign. We'll cover all of this in greater detail later in the book. The goal of this chapter is for you to jot down some notes so that as we move forward you can build on that foundation.

# SECTION 3:
# UNDERSTAND

CHAPTER 5

# Metrics

There are a number of metrics that you need to know how to calculate in order to create a successful data-driven marketing campaign. Most of these data points are calculated inside your analytics platform, but it is still good to know the components of each.

This chapter will help you define the primary metrics of any data-driven marketing campaign and help you understand how to use these metrics in your strategy.

## Key Metrics

Understanding how to calculate these metrics will give you more control over your campaign. In most cases, you can pull these data points automatically from your analytics or CRM platform. Let's review each metric so you have the knowledge needed to setup your campaign.

**Cost per Impression**

*Traffic Cost (by channel) / Impressions*

**Cost per Click**

*Traffic Cost (by channel) / Clicks*

**Cost per Cookie**

*Remarketing Traffic Cost / Clicks (or tracked cookies)*

**Cost per Lead**

*Total Campaign Cost / Number of Leads*

**Cost per Contact (List Buy)**

This metric is typically used when buying a list.
*Cost of the list / the number of contacts on the list*

**Cost per Company (List Buy)**

This is another metric used when buying a list.
*Cost of the list / the number of companies on the list*

### How to set a target cost per lead when planning

It's always a good idea to create a target cost per lead when planning your campaign. This will give you an initial target to aim for. As you move from campaign to campaign, you'll get a better idea of what this value should be. Continually improving this metric will typically lead to higher ROI overall. Just don't get too caught up on this metric. It's only part of your overall success.

### Cost per Acquisition (Sale)

*Total Cost of Campaign / Number of New Customers*

### How to set a target cost per acquisition when planning

Calculating a goal CPA is done based on some of the known metrics of your business.

*Example:*
- *Company XYZ sells a product that is $12,000 per year*
- *They are looking to acquire 10 new customers in Q1*
- *They are willing to spend $2000 to acquire a new customer*
- *Based on these metrics they are budgeting $20,000 to generate $120,000 in revenue*

This example goes a little beyond just calculating CPA. This is a great example of how all of these metrics start to come together.

## Campaign ROI

*Gross Sales / Total Campaign Cost*

## How to set a target campaign ROI

Continuing from the example in calculating CPA we have:
- *Gross Sales $120,000 / Total Campaign Cost $20,000*
- *Campaign ROI = 600%*

If we were to keep the same assumptions, our target ROI would be 600%, or for every $1 we put into the campaign, we would expect to get $6 back.

## Monthly Lead Stage Conversion Rates

It is also important to measure the conversion rate between stages in your lead funnel. This can help you over time to isolate issues in your sales efforts. Once you've completed a few campaigns, you should have well-documented conversion rates between stages. If a new campaign isn't performing as well as you would like, it is important to have a comparison point to isolate where the break down is happening.

## Prospect to MQL

*Number of Prospects at start of period /*
*Number of prospects that become MQL in time period*

*Example:*
- *At the start of the month we had 100 prospects*
- *10 of those prospects become MQL's*
- *100 / 10 = 10% Prospect to MQL Conversion Rate*

## MQL to SQL

*Number of MQL at start of period /*
*Number of MQL that become SQL in time period*

*Example:*
- *At the start of the month we had 10 MQL*
- *5 of those MQL become SQL's*
- *10 / 5 = 50% MQL to SQL Conversion Rate*

### SQL to Opportunity

*Number of SQL at start of period /*
*Number of SQL that become Opportunities in time period*

*Example:*
- *At the start of the month we had 5 SQL*
- *2 of those SQL become Opportunities*
- *5 / 2 = 20% SQL to Opportunity Conversion Rate*

### Opp to Win

*Number of Opportunities at start of period /*
*Number of Opportunities that convert to sales in time period*

*Example:*
- *At the start of the month we had 2 Opportunities*
- *1 of those Opportunities buys*
- *2 / 1 = 50% Opportunity to Win Rate*

## Opp to Loss

*Number of Opportunities at start of period /*
*Number of Opportunities that we lose in time period*

*Example:*

- *At the start of the month we had 2 Opportunities*
- *1 of those Opportunities decides not to buy (full loss with no potential future opportunity)*
- *2 / 1 = 50% Loss Rate*

I used round numbers to make the math easier. Hopefully at this point you can see how all of the numbers feed into the overall campaign statistics.

*Important Note: When calculating conversion rates over a month, it's important to keep your initial figures static. If you start to include leads that move between stages into the initial monthly numbers, it's easy to get lost in your calculations.

# CHAPTER 6

# Setting Up Your Sales Cycle

Earlier in the book, we gave you an introduction to each of the sales cycle stages. In this chapter, we're going to review those stages and talk about how a lead enters the sales stage and some of the activities that cause the lead to leave the sales stage.

This chapter will help you define your nurturing process, or your sales cycle. In other words, we are going to break down the steps needed in the sales cycle for you to apply to your own strategy.

By the end of this chapter, you should be ready to set up your lead stages in your CRM.

We are going to start by reviewing each stage. This is a critically important element of any data-driven marketing campaign. Remember, data-driven marketing is also referred to as 'database marketing', so you need to make absolutely certain your database (CRM) is in order.

## Lead Stage: Contact

A contact is anyone on your list that has not been qualified because they do not have the needed data or do not align with your persona. We place 'leads' in this bucket to signify that there is a data need before any sales or marketing efforts are applied to the lead.

### Entry Points

Data is added to your contact list one of two ways. Either it is uploaded at the onset of a campaign as previous campaign data or as a purchased list. Contacts can also be added from lead generation activities. If you're running an Inbound Campaign where you're not certain of the contact's qualification status, it's best to add them to the contact list until you can qualify them based on your persona.

### Exit Points

Contacts leave this list a few different ways:
- They are qualified through to a Prospect
- They are disqualified and removed from the campaign
- You are unable to qualify them through data mining, data purchase, or contact

### Things to Look Out For

The best way to work on your contact list is to purchase the missing data needed to qualify them. If you're unable to do that, the next option would be to try to data mine their information either from LinkedIn or their website. If that still doesn't work, then just leave them on this list until you've exhausted all other leads from all other lead stages.

## Lead Stage: Prospect

A prospect is a lead who matches all five of your persona elements. This is a critical definition that can save you an amazing amount of time and money. The second biggest waste in any funnel (after poor ad spend) is the time spent working on leads that were never qualified. You can eliminate that by keeping leads in the contact bucket until they have persona match. You can then move them to the prospect list.

The prospect list is where your marketing begins. Now that they are qualified from a data perspective, it is time to engage them. As leads will come from different sources, the next step can have a couple different paths. We'll get more into those when we talk about implementing your campaigns.

### Entry Points

A qualified contact

### Exit Points

There is a very high drop off rate here. This is the initial point of engagement so you're going to end up talking to just as many leads that are interested in moving forward as you are ones that are not.

**Things to Look Out For**

If you're dealing in with a large amount of prospects, it's best to automate this part of your campaign. Leverage emails and social engagement to trigger an activity on your site. Make sure that your CRM is set up to send a notification as soon as a prospect visits an important page on your site. This will trigger a direct reach out.

# Lead Stage: Marketing Qualified Lead (MQL)

A Marketing Qualified Lead (MQL) is a prospect that has been engaged. Engagement means they have responded in some way to a marketing message that shows some level of interest in your offer. This can be a response to an email, the completion of a long form on your site, or attendance to a paid event. This doesn't necessarily show they are ready to buy. It just shows that they are engaged.

This is an important stage. This is the point where the marketing team is now ready to turn the lead over to sales. If the marketing team can qualify and engage a lead to this point of interest, the next step is to turn them into a Sales Qualified Lead.

**Entry Points**

Engaged Prospect

## Exit Points

There is still a lot of drop off at this stage. This is the critical handoff between marketing and sales.

### Things to Look Out For

In a new data-driven marketing organization, you have to be conscious of the technical and procedural handoff between teams. There are a lot of ways leads can get lost in this process. If your qualification and engagements skills are strong, sales should be more than happy to pick up right where marketing left off.

# Lead Stage: Sales Qualified Lead (SQL)

A Sales Qualified Lead (SQL) is an MQL that has completed an initial discovery call and that has expressed interest in continuing the sales conversation.

### Entry Points

SQLs come from MQLs that have voluntarily completed a discovery process and are now waiting on a proposal.

### Exit Points

This stage can go a lot of different directions. When a lead reaches the SQL stage, we tend to give them a 50% close rate. We've generated interest and delivered our offer. Now we have to work to keep them moving forward. Leads should not sit on this list for long.

**Things to Look Out For**

Some sales reps get trigger-happy here and move MQLs to SQLs when they schedule their sales conversation. That's a bit too early. You need to complete the sales conversation to a point where both parties are interested in moving to the proposal process.

# Lead Stage: Opportunity

We're now one step away from ringing that bell. A lead moves to the Opportunity stage the moment they acknowledge receipt of your proposal. You've completed the qualification, engagement, and discovery. Now all that is left for you to do is close the deal. Keeping this lead stage up to date is easy because it's where the majority of your future revenue sits.

**Entry Points**

A delivered proposal

**Exit Points**

From here, the lead typically moves to the win stage or the loss stage.

**Things to Look Out For**

I've always made sure that my sales reps understand that we don't ring the bell until we have processed the payment. A signed contract is great, but show me the money!

## Lead Stage: Won

This one is pretty straightforward. When you sign the contract and deposit the check, you can mark the lead as won. This is the 'ring the bell' moment that we all work towards. This doesn't mean the sales process is over, but for the sake of this discussion, it's the critical point of success.

### Entry Points

This is pretty straightforward. You have a signed contract and you've received payment. Go ring that bell!

### Exit Points

Inside any given campaign, once someone buys they tend to stay on the win list until there is a contract expiration where they do not renew. Then they can be moved back to an appropriate stage based on their reason for not renewing.

They may also be moved from the win list to a new campaign if your service offering has changed enough to warrant reengaging with the lead on a new sales contact.

### Things to Look Out For

Always be thinking upsell. Each time you have a new offer, contact your current customers first to see their interest. You're eight times more likely to generate additional revenue from a current customer than you are to sell a new customer.

## Lead Stage: Loss

You win some, you lose some. In fact, we all lose a lot (if you're trying, that is). This lead stage is for deals that didn't close. That doesn't mean this is a dead lead. It just means you didn't win this round. We'll leave the lead here until we can trigger an activity to move it back out again.

### Entry Points

You've gone through the entire sales process and you get confirmation they have purchased from someone else. This is not a soft no list. This is a firm "not going to buy from you" signal.

### Exit Points

The reason we use this lead stage is so that if you come to market with a new offer, you have a list of people that made it through your sales stages but did not buy. Reach out to them with the new offer to see if there is an alignment opportunity.

### Things to Look Out For

Sales reps can spend too much time on a dead opportunity. Be cautious, but also be willing to move leads to the loss column.

## Lead Stage: Do Not Contact

From time to time we run into that pain in the ass that ever so politely tells you to get lost. This stage is reserved for those people that have made it super clear that they don't want anything to do with you AND you agree that it is not worth your time to pursue them. This stage should be used as little as possible. This is where leads go to die.

### Entry Points

A firm "do not contact me" or spam report on a previous email. Some sales reps still see that as a challenge. I see it as an indicator to move on to someone ready and willing to talk to you about doing business.

### Exit Points

It's rare, but from time to time people will ask you not to contact them, and then you'll see them visit your site. Make sure to have a notification set up in your CRM anytime someone on your do not contact list visits your site.

### Things to Look Out For

Keep an eye out for these people both visiting your site and at live events. You're always looking for that point of reengagement.

## Lead Stage: Cold Lead

We typically reserve this stage for a lead that has gone 180 days without a response to at least ten attempts to contact. These attempts must include at least one of each of the following: Email, Social Media (like LinkedIn), and a phone call. A great way for a sales rep to lose their job in an organization we work with is for them to place a lead in the cold lead stage because they didn't respond to a handful of emails. Pick up the phone and make sure they are still out there.

### Entry Points

We tend to move leads to this list if we go more than 180 days without contact.

### Exit Points

When our sales teams are up to date on all of the current leads and opportunities, we have them go back through this list. We try to make sure that we contact this list via email and phone at least once per month.

### Things to Look Out For

People move jobs (change emails and phone numbers), so a great place to find a cold lead is on LinkedIn. Their profile tends to stay the same even when they change jobs. Never let a sales representative move someone to a cold lead based on email history alone.

## Lead Stage: Future Follow up

The larger the deal you're working, the more likely you are to run into annual budgets, current contracts, or cycles that are beyond your control. It's best to document those issues and move the lead over to the future follow up stage. You would also want to add a trigger to notify you as to when you should reach back out.

### Entry Points

Leads are moved to this stage only when a predetermined and agreed upon date is given for follow up. This typically happens when you have an interested buyer that is restricted by a fiscal budget or an expiring current contract.

## Exit Points

When properly managed, leads should be taken off of this list and moved back to their previous qualification stage when their follow up date arrives. Depending on how far they were into the buying process before they reached a date-based impasse will reflect where you move them back to.

## Things to Look Out For

You always want to keep an eye on this list. It's easy to miss opportunities that are on this list. Always make sure to set a reminder in your CRM so you get a notification when it's time to follow up with a lead on your list.

# CHAPTER 7

# Finding Your Customer

Where does your ideal buyer persona like to hang out? We will approach this from a macro point of view in order to try to simplify your initial targeting. We will cover some of the major platforms that we use in our business in order to engage with and convert our ideal buyer into a lead and then into a paying client.

There are numerous platforms to choose from and every industry has one that works best for it. These are some of our favorite, and some of the easiest, ones to engage with right out of the gate.

## Facebook

With over one billion active daily users, there's a high probability that your ideal buyer spends some time on Facebook. We have found this to be true in the majority of the campaigns we have run over the last few years with only a few exceptions. Those exceptions tend to be audiences that we will find on the next platform, LinkedIn.

Facebook gives you numerous targeting capabilities. Inside their advertising platform, they've broken down and segmented a lot of targeting capabilities that allow you to show your ads only to your ideal buyer. Their ad platform sophistication has grown over the years and has made it very easy to come to market with a limited budget to create initial engagement.

Another great strategy for engaging your ideal buyer on Facebook is to participate in groups that other organizations have started. This will allow you to catch the pulse of your ideal buyer's community so that you can strategically engage with them through answering their questions and offering advice on their success. It's wise not to make direct offers in other people's groups, but instead to build conversations one-on-one so they can eventually lead to an opportunity to sell.

## LinkedIn

LinkedIn is a great place to connect with your ideal buyer if you are in an enterprise B2B space. Our experience has been that this can include buyer personas in software and healthcare. There are numerous other ideal buyer personas that you can also find on LinkedIn.

Just as with Facebook, LinkedIn groups are great way to leverage one-on-one conversations with your ideal buyer in an environment where you can offer advice and position yourself as an expert.

We typically leverage LinkedIn through LinkedIn Sales Navigator so that we can find our ideal buyer and reach out to them one-on-one with an initial offer. When done correctly, the LinkedIn platform can be your primary source for B2B leads.

## Trade Shows/Events

This has always been one of my favorite ways to engage with a target audience. When we ran services in the nonprofit space, we had no better conversion than sponsoring and putting a tradeshow booth at some of the major nonprofit conferences each year. Although they are expensive, they tend to have the best direct contact with decision-makers and the highest possible ROI in the shortest period of time.

Some additional strategies for engaging your ideal buyer through the use of tradeshows is to acquire a list of everyone that is attending the event as far in advance as the event organizers will make it available. You will most likely have to pay extra for this list if they do not provide a platform for engaging with the audience. One of the things that Microsoft does very well is creating online communities around their annual conferences. This allows you to directly reach out to the individuals that are attending the event to try to create initial interest in conversations before you arrive.

## List Buys

We typically reserve campaign list buys for organizations that have a mature outbound sales department. The idea that you can buy a cold email list and then convert those cold leads into paying customers at a higher rate is unlikely. We found that it takes a combination of outbound email, as well as outbound telesales, to engage a cold list with any level of success. This is an oversimplification of creating ROI from list buys, but it should point out the complexity of doing this.

## Cross Platform

You may find that your ideal buyer spends time on a lot of different platforms. This may require you to engage with them across different platforms at different times. It's still important for you to pick a primary platform in which to initially engage with them. This allows you to start the conversation and then let the conversation flow through all of the other platforms naturally.

A good example of this is in our own business is that we will engage with individuals on LinkedIn in preparation for a trade show. We do our initial outreach in order to create a conversation and then invite them to our booth and/or any special event that we might do at the trade show in order to start to build a relationship with the individual. Your ability to leverage cross-platform engagement will be directly proportional to your ability to drive ROI from each of your campaigns.

This is by no means meant to be an all-encompassing list. These are simply the strategies that we use in our campaigns to target buyers for our own products and our clients.

In the next chapter, we're going to talk about how to test the different platforms that you use to target your ideal buyer during the launch phase. This will give you an opportunity to analyze and make adjustments as needed.

# SECTION 4:
# DECIDE & AUTOMATE

# CHAPTER 8

# Goals

Setting goals in a data-driven marketing campaign follow the same principles of setting goals on any other type of marketing campaign.

Before we define the data-driven marketing campaign goals, I would like to review overall goal setting. It's an underutilized business fundamental that is the primary problem why most organizations fail to grow.

## Setting goals

The lack of goal setting inside organizations is typically worse inside digital marketing agencies. Most of the agencies that I've worked with struggle to grow because they don't set realistic goals in their business and then they don't implement their own services on their own company. This is called eating your own dog food. You don't literally eat your dog food, but do you always implement the services that you provide your customers in your own organization for proof of concept and easy conversation points about the success that you had utilizing those service?

Goal setting can be broken down into five parts. Let's review each of those and then we will outline how those parts work in conjunction with the data-driven marketing campaign.

First, define your goal. This sounds simple, but it's often overlooked. What exactly do you expect the outcome of your campaign to be? This is not a generalization. This needs to be an exact target number. This can be reflected in the number of net new customers. It can be reflected in the amount of net new Revenue. Whatever it is, it needs to be an exact and definable statistical element. More often than not, the goal will be based off of one primary KPI that we covered earlier in the book.

The second element of a goal is to set the date in which the goal will be reached. This is an exact date. It's not a few months from now, it's not a few weeks from now, it's not next year. It's a date like February 12, 2018.

The reason for an exact date is to make sure that there is absolute accountability when the goal is supposed to be reached. If you do not have an exact date for your goal to hold you accountable, there is a high probability you'll never reach your goal. They should be reflected both in the campaigns that you do internally in your organization as an agency, as well as in the campaigns that you implement for your clients. This will help you to retain clients and higher monthly retainers by being transparent in your activities and the dates that you will deliver results.

The third part in setting a goal is to define the exact strategy you will use. This will include all of the elements that have been covered in this book up to this point (technology, data, marketing channels, and go-to-market strategies). Define these in detail and cover all of the implementation elements that will be included in this goal.

The fourth part of goal setting is to benchmark success KPIs. Once your campaign is broken down into implementation sections, it's important to define how your KPIs will grow overtime. This can start with measuring the amount of traffic that's being driven from a specific channel all the way through to conversion metrics It will let you know if the channels are performing the way that you want them to perform. By setting these benchmark APIs, you will learn to evaluate and adjust your campaign as time moves on in order to optimize to reach your predetermined goal.

The last part of goal setting is implementation, review, analysis, and adjustments. With a well-defined goal that includes defined KPIs built around a defined strategy, it will be easy to measure the success of your campaign at each stage. This may lead to adjusting specific elements of your implementation strategy in order to best optimize your efforts to help reach your goal of the predetermined completion date.

No campaign is ever implemented without adjustments to some elements. The better defined your overall goals and strategy, the easier it will be for you to make the adjustments necessary to reach your goals with greater probability.

Without defined goals and strategy, you are not ready to start implementation. Let's go through an example goal setting strategy for a data-driven marketing campaign.

## Step One – Setting the Goal

*Example:*
*We are going to implement an email campaign to generate two new customers for our analytics platform in the next 30 days.*

So what is wrong with this example?

First, it's not exact. What do those two new customers actually mean from a revenue perspective? Second, "in the next 30 days" doesn't define a date in which to do it. It would be too easy to say that the campaign was launched on one day, get two weeks in, and then decide instead to launch it now. By having a variable term of next 30 days, you're not holding yourself accountable to any specific deadline.

*Revised example:*
*Our goal is to close two new analytics customers at $500 per month to a 12-month contract by February 17, 2018.*

This is an exact goal that states what the outcome of this campaign will be and the date that we will reach it.

As you can see in the example above, we both set our goal and provided a deadline to reach that goal. This is very common in the initial strategy session for goal setting.

The next step is to define a strategy.

*Example:*
*We will use Facebook traffic to create trial conversions to a landing page on our website.*

What is wrong with this strategy?

Let's start with what's right in the strategy. We did define our traffic source and we did define our conversion point.

So what did we fail to define?

We failed to set a budget for the amount of traffic we were going to buy. We did not define what type of Facebook traffic we were going to be doing. Also, if we are going to use the trial offer as a tripwire, we did not define how that tripwire will convert into a paying customer.

*Revised example:*
*We are going to spend $2000 on Facebook advertising to drive clicks from promoted posts to our website offer of a trial. We are going to generate 20 trial conversions at a cost of $100 per trial with the goal of converting two of those trial offers into monthly paying customers.*

That gives us the basis of a macro strategy. We want to break that down even further into the individual elements to make sure we have a complete understanding of each stage of this process.

This could include elements such as split testing landing pages, split testing auto responders, and then also driving into our sales funnel to make sure that our implementation and conversion process generate the revenue that we're looking for.

The next step is to set the primary KPI's that we're going to measure. There are a lot of different primary statistics that we could look at we're going to cover three macro statistics that should be part of every campaign as part of this example.

*Example:*
*Budget $2000*
*Cost per trial user $100*
*Cost per conversion $1000*

Each of these elements can be broken down further into the cost per click, the click through rate, and other statistical elements that would help us to find these macro budget elements. In your goal setting, it's most important to cover your macro numbers and then let the campaign drive the micro numbers that are used to benchmark your overall goals.

It's now time to implement and to review our strategy. We have taken the time to define our goal, set a deadline, create a strategy, and outline our primary KPIs. All that is left is to do is to implement and review our strategy as we work towards our goal.

For a 30-day campaign, it's a good idea to break this down into weekly benchmarks so that we can track our progress throughout the campaign.

Every organization is different and every offer is different. It's important for you to understand the length of the sales cycle related to the product that you're selling.

The product, using the example above, has an instant conversion to a trial offer that then leads to a 14-day trial that typically converts within a day or two at the end of the trial. This is a fairly easy B2B product to generate a funnel for. If you have an enterprise or high-ticket offer, this process may be longer, or it may even be shorter. We'll talk more about that in the Sales Cycle section of this book.

An overall strategy goal setting session might go a little bit more in depth than this. If done correctly at the level of which we covered in this book, you will find it much easier to set and reach goals in your own campaigns as well as in your client campaigns.

# CHAPTER 9

# Choosing the Right Technology

Technology plays a critical role in any data-driven marketing campaign. You need to have a house for all of your data and systems to process the data.

There are thousands to choose from, but I'm just going to give you some of the top choices that I've worked with in the past.

## Customer Relationship Manager (CRM)

A CRM is where you house all of your contact data so that you can manage your overall sales efforts.

Some of the most popular tools that I have worked with in the past are listed below.

**Salesforce**: I would not recommend this to the everyday user because it's an enterprise solution. It's complicated to set up, but it has a lot of advanced functionality and integration capabilities necessary for the success of enterprise organizations.

www.Salesforce.com

**Microsoft Dynamics CRM**: This is Microsoft's attempt to play in the CRM market. Although statistically they have great penetration in the market, this is not one of the easier tools to use. It's well adopted in the SMB space and is a great solution for those already using the suite of Microsoft Products.

www.Microsoft.com/en-us/Dynamics365/What-is-crm

**HubSpot CRM**: They have a completely free version that is great for small business and gives you the opportunity to learn how to use a CRM. HubSpot's CRM also integrates with their marketing automation platform that I'll talk a little bit more about in the next section.

www.HubSpot.com/Products/crm

There are a lot of other CRM platforms out there, some of which are great tools that I've never tried to use before; others can end up just being a time suck. If you're looking for the best CRM for you, take a look online at the different features that a

CRM offers. Use free trials in order to get used to them and then pick the one that best fits your business needs.

The reality is that a CRM is only as good as the effort that you put into it. Too often, the best technology is left sitting on the shelf because we don't apply the time needed to learn how to use it and/or officially keep our data updated in the platform.

## Marketing Automation Platform

These are tools that integrate contact data with email and marketing capabilities. These can include the ability to set up landing pages to use forms, order set up, email workflows, and automated funnels. They are critical piece of data-driven marketing. Listed below are some of the tools that we have used.

**SharpSpring** is one of my favorites. It's not the most robust, but it has all of the basic capabilities needed to implement successful sales and marketing automation campaigns. It has one of the lowest fee structures of any platform on the market, which makes it very attractive in the SMB space.

https://SharpSpring.com/

**HubSpot** would probably be my favorite platform except for the cost. Depending on the number of contacts that you have in your database and the amount of reach that you do to that database, HubSpot can get very expensive. It has a lot of great tools and has come a long way with their reporting platform in order to give you a powerful tool to manage all of your sales and marketing elements. This also has a seamless integration with HubSpot CRM which makes it a powerful tool.

www.HubSpot.com

**ClickDimensions** is a very popular marketing automation tool in the Microsoft space. It's direct integration into dynamics CRM give the market dominance space in the Microsoft ecosystem. It's a very clunky system and very hard to use relative to its competition. They've done a lot of work over the past few years to improve performance, but it's not a recommended tool for users outside of dynamics CRM.

www.ClickDimensions.com

**InfusionSoft** is a marketing automation platform that is very popular in the digital marketing and affiliate marketing space. It's slightly different than the tools mentioned above as it's not necessarily a robust sales automation tool in the B2B sales environment, but what it lacks in that environment, it makes up for in its shopping cart and e-commerce platform capabilities. It's always been considered a complicated tool to learn, but they have made strides over the past few years improving the UI and UX elements of the platform.

**SalsaLabs** is a marketing automation platform specifically designed for the nonprofit industry. It's one of the better tools serving that space based on the fact that all of its competitors have been bought out by the same company that has zero concern for customer service or improving their technology past it's 2000 peek. That might sound a little harsh, but if you're in the nonprofit space, stick with SalsaLabs and you'll save yourself a lot of time and headaches.

www.SalsaLabs.com/

Just as with CRM tools, there are numerous marketing automation platforms out there to choose from. Most marketing automation platforms offer a free trial that I would highly recommend you taking advantage of before committing to an annual contract which could range anywhere from $100 per month to upwards of $2500 per month depending on the level of usage and functionality that you're looking for.

## Analytics Tools

It's highly recommended that every website use Google analytics. There really is no better tool in the SMB space as it's free and it gives you some of the most robust information that you could ever need when it comes to marketing.

www.Google.com/Analytics

As a digital marketing agency or as a marketer that is using multiple tools at once, I would check out agency analytics as a great way to pull all of your data together into one platform so that you can get a clear picture of what's going on across all of your different efforts in campaigns.

As machine learning is becoming more prominent in the data analytics side of the marketing world, there are other tools out there that can give you great insight into opportunities that humans just can't process on their own.

In the SMB space, I would highly recommend taking a look at Enfusen not only because it's my company, but also because we've designed it to integrate all of your data sources into one seamless stream which we then analyze against hundreds of thousands of campaign strategies to make recommendations to help you drive traffic and conversion for your clients.

https://www.enfusen.com/

Enterprise users can check out the Adobe Marketing Cloud which can run as much as $50,000 per year for one website, but this is definitely a case of you get what you pay for. Its advanced predictive analytics elements are what separate industry leaders from the rest of the enterprise organizations.

http://www.Adobe.com/Marketing-Cloud.html

As a data-driven marketer, you will also need tools to help you cleanse and enrich your data. Below are the two data providers we use in our own business for this.

## Data Brokers

If you're looking to cleanse and enrich B2B data, I highly recommend NetProspex. They were acquired a few years ago by Dun & Bradstreet and are definitely one of the top providers of B2B data in the industry. Their seamless and easy-to-use API functionality allows you to connect your current data to their tool so that you can cleanse and enrich your data in a matter of minutes. They may cost you a little bit of money, but it's a highly recommend option for keeping your data updated.

https://www.Netprospex.com

In the B2C space, the best provider is Tower Data. They again give you a seamless interface to upload your list to be cleansed and enriched for all of the different data that you could think of relating to consumer behavior. They go as far as being able to tell you magazine subscriptions, donation history, family size, household information and a lot of other relevant information that can help you to create strategically targeted campaigns to your B2C list.

http://www.TowerData.com

A lot of these tools can be combined into a single platform fairly easily. This is called an all-in-one tool. By combining your CRM and your marketing automation elements into one seamless tool, you can eliminate data mistakes and optimize automation opportunities.

When looking for a top all-in-one tool that contain CRM marketing automation and some type of analytics I would definitely recommend taking a look at SharpSpring first and then also HubSpot. Between those two, you should be able to find a solution that you're looking for.

# SECTION 5:
# EXECUTE

# Integrate

Now that we've defined all of our data points, chosen our technology, and set our goals, it's time to put all the pieces together. This is a critical part of the process that, if done correctly, will make your life a lot easier going forward.

## Integrating Your Technology

I'll walk through each tool that you're going to use in this process and the basics of how you set it up to ensure your data is properly structured and ready for your campaign.

## Integrating Your Data

The first thing that we're going to do is upload our contact data into our CRM or marketing automation platform. This is a critical step to make sure that we properly map our dataset so when we go to use the data, we have all of the available columns that are needed properly target our audience. Most platforms make this process easy so that you can upload a .csv file that will pull the column headers and properly map the data for you.

In order for this process to go smoothly, try not to create too many custom columns in your very first upload. The most important thing at this point is to get the basic contact data into your platform and properly mapped so that you can begin to run a campaign. This includes all of the basic data elements that are part of building your buyer persona that were outlined earlier in the book.

## Integrating Your Analytics

Next you want to integrate and/or add any needed analytics codes in order to be able to track your campaign success. Many tools allow you to integrate Google Analytics directly into their platform. Other tools may have their own analytics code you will need to install on your website. It's important not to skip over this step because you'll need to be able to measure engagement data to properly implement a data-driven marketing campaign. Most platforms provide exact instructions. If you aren't comfortable doing this, reach out to your web developer who can do it pretty easily for you.

## Mapping Your Email

When setting up new marketing automation platforms or email marketing platforms, ensure the platform signatures are properly set up so you have high deliverability rates. Tools like SharpSpring have a panel where you can easily enter a few data points that will allow you to connect your email IP address with the platform IP address to improve deliverability. Contact whatever platform you're working with to make sure that this is properly mapped and do not skip over this point. Every platform we worked with has tutorials on how to do this to help guide the process.

## Connecting Your Marketing Automation Platform with Your CRM

If you're not going to be using an all-in-one platform, you'll also want to integrate your CRM with your marketing automation platform in order to share data between the two. One of the most common problems that we ran into during the research phase of this book was organizations that used non-connected marketing tools and sales tools. There is no reason to be using tools that are not connected and sharing data. It only creates a burden in your business to try to run campaigns between unconnected systems.

## Other Possible Integrations

Depending on the type of funnel that you're going to be running and the technology platform that you've chosen, there may be other elements that you want to integrate. Below is a list of some of the more common platforms that fall outside of data-driven marketing, but may be critical to your campaign's success.

**Shopping Cart**: If you're running e-commerce campaigns and you're not on Infusionsoft, you may need to integrate your shopping cart into your marketing automation platform to properly track sales.

**Payment Processor**: If you're an e-commerce seller, or even a service provider, it's typically a good idea to integrate your payment processing tool with your marketing automation platform so you can not only track the point of conversion, but also record revenue generated for metrics in the future.

**Support Desk**: Many organizations like Saas Providers or e-commerce sellers may have a support desk that they want to integrate directly with their CRM so they can track support tickets in relation to sales and customer retention.

Many of the all-in-one tools available today will also allow you to integrate social media so you can track engagement from social media through your site into your CRM conversion points.

There are plenty of other integrations that can be done depending on the complexity of your campaign. These are just a few of the main elements that we use in our campaigns.

As technology advances, the ability to integrate more of our efforts into one seamless platform will help us all to be more successful marketers.

# CHAPTER 11

# Marketing

No book on data-driven marketing would be complete without a review of the most common digital marketing channels. A simple Google search will turn up lists with as many as 80 different digital marketing channels to consider when putting together a marketing campaign. I'm going to list the ones that we most commonly use when implementing our campaigns for our organization and for our clients.

# My Favorite Digital Marketing Channels

### Search Engine Optimization (SEO)

Search engine optimization is the process of optimizing the website in order to rank organically in the search engines for specific search phrases. This has long been one of my favorite channels and is considered one of the most efficient channels when done right.

Search engine optimization can play an important role in data-driven marketing campaigns. Its integration with content marketing can create powerful lead generation funnels that feed directly into your CRM and sales funnel activities.

## Search Engine Marketing (SEM or PPC)

Search engine marketing, or pay-per-click, is the process of paying a search engine or site when people engage with your ads or content. The most common platforms for pay-per-click marketing are Google AdWords and Facebook marketing. There are numerous opportunities to do paid traffic through platforms like LinkedIn, Twitter, Snapchat, Instagram, or even directly with other websites or search engines.

Just as search engine optimization plays an important role in data-driven marketing, search engine marketing can be a critical piece to coming to market with a new offer and creating leads that feed into your data-driven marketing campaign.

## Social Selling

There are a lot of different ways to leverage social media as part of the data-driven marketing campaign. I choose to focus on social selling. This is different than posting to social media to syndicate content and create brand awareness. This is the intentional act of engaging with individuals and social media with a direct sales funnel in order to convert them into a paying customer.

In B2B data-driven marketing, my favorite source for social selling is LinkedIn. LinkedIn provides numerous tools like the LinkedIn Sales Navigator that allow you to do in-depth research on potential leads and create conversations inside the platform driving people to a sales conversation and eventual conversion point.

## Content Marketing

Content marketing can take a lot of different forms ranging from blog posting, resource creation, or a combination of strategies that are all built around inbound marketing. Numerous books have been written primarily on content marketing strategies that make this a very broad topic for an in-depth analysis in this book.

Content is one of the critical pieces of all data-driven marketing strategies. From crafting landing page copy, blog posts, and resource offers, to educating your potential buyer on the value of your products and services, content marketing will play a critical role in your campaign.

## Email Marketing

A cornerstone of data-driven marketing is the use of email marketing. Your ability to engage your prospects in order to start conversations via email is one of the primary drivers of campaign success. It's also a critical piece of nurturing

104 · ROGER BRYAN

relationships to continue the creation and syndication of educational content.

With the average individual receiving well over 100 marketing emails per week, it's important to be able to craft a message that not only gets into the reader's inbox, but also gets opened and consumed in a competitive engagement. The art of writing emails has become much more sophisticated over the years. You will need to master this art or find a resource that can help you leverage email marketing to implement successful data-driven marketing campaigns.

## Public Relations (PR)

Public relations (PR) is the process of leveraging authority websites to create brand awareness as well as create traffic back to your primary offer. PR is also a great way to leverage credibility in your other marketing efforts. Getting a high-value placement on Inc. Magazine or Entrepreneur Magazine's website gives you great content that you can send out to your potential leads in order to showcase your position in the market.

A big part of our data-driven marketing is continuing a conversation with your prospects as they move through your lead stages. A high-value PR placement is a great way to reengage leads that have stalled or that have not converted in the past. Your potential customers are looking to work with industry leaders. High-quality PR can put you in that position of authority and help you to convert more paying customers.

## Video Marketing

Video marketing has become one of my favorite lead generation strategies. Video can be leveraged through a combination of the above strategies. A well-crafted video can be syndicated across social media. You can use paid traffic to create engagement with your videos, where they can be placed on your website and properly optimized to generate organic traffic. This is a great example of how all of these marketing channel strategies can be used in combination.

A big part of data-driven marketing is leveraging your understanding of the customer based on the data that you have in your system to analyze for opportunity. That data can often lead to a better understanding of what content you create to move people through the stages of your lead funnel. There's no better way to do this than through educational content or educational videos that showcase your understanding of the unique problems of your potential customers.

## Remarketing (Retargeting)

Even though remarketing has now been around for the better part of a decade, it's still one of the most underutilized marketing channels that I know of. When organizations apply the same amount of time, energy, and resources to creating large databases of cookied, previously engaged potential customers as they do with building their email list, they tend to see a great deal of financial return from those efforts.

Remarketing is the process of tagging people who engage with your content so that you can target them with future content. The entire premise of data-driven marketing is having an understanding of your target audience and an ability to engage them at different points in order to drive them towards a predetermined conversion point.

## Community Building

Community building is the process of determining your target customer and then building a captive audience by leveraging one of the many different social platforms that allow you to do this. In recent years, I've seen that the most successful marketers are those that understand community building.

One great example of this is building Facebook groups that are private and require registration. If this captive audience is properly engaged and educated, it can be a great source of revenue for organizations that take the time to build and maintain relationships with its members.

While there are dozens of other digital marketing channels to consider, these are the primary channels that we leverage in our own campaigns and in campaigns for our customers. I recommend that you master one channel before you move on to another. Any one of these channels, once mastered, can provide an almost endless supply of new leads and new sales opportunities. Where most people struggle is trying to master them all and become a master of none.

# CHAPTER 12

# Launch

It's day one of your campaign and you're about to click the proverbial button to make it live. Depending on your go-to-market strategy, this could be a literal button or it could be a figurative button. The content is created, your funnel is in place, your technology is set up, and you're about to turn on the traffic.

What are the best implementation strategies for launching a successful campaign? That's what we will cover in this chapter.

We like to break our campaigns into 90-day cycles. This allows us to strategically build models around each element of implementation. The three cycles that we run are Test, Optimize, and Convert. We have found that these three cycles can be applied to any marketing channel.

The amount of time that you will spend on each of these cycles is directly dependent upon your experience targeting your audience in promoting your current offer. If this is the first campaign you have run for this offer and the first time that you've ever targeted this buyer persona, you may spend more time in the first phase than you would if you had a greater amount of experience in the space. It's critical that as you run through the cycles that you aggressively watch each of your metrics and take notes about what impacts those metrics both positively and negatively. Successful data-driven marketers are always paying attention to the metrics and trying to learn as much from them as possible to help them with future activities.

We've defined our goal, we've defined our go-to-market strategy, we defined our sales cycle, and now we're ready to start to drive traffic into our campaign. This leads us up into the first cycle of our launch. We call this the test cycle.

## Test Cycle

In the test cycle, we are looking to see if we can connect with our ideal customer. We plot this as a 30-day cycle, but it can be a much shorter depending on how well we defined our strategy and how well we understand our ideal buyer. In this cycle, we are beginning to slowly spend our budget trying to create engagement with our ideal buyer. Here are a few things we do in our test cycle.

We start by testing and targeting. Do we have a wide enough audience to drive to our overall campaign goal? We can typically see this pretty quickly. Are we getting enough impressions to match the metrics that we've drawn up in our overall campaign strategy? If you're struggling to get the number of impressions, we may have picked the wrong go-to-market strategy or the wrong marketing channel. If the audience is not there, it's time to reconfigure our targeting so that we can move onto the next cycle.

The opposite of not having a large enough audience is having too wide of an audience. Are we starting to see engagement from individuals that are obviously not our ideal buyer? This can happen when the leads are coming in from individuals that have no intent or capability to buy our product. If you're running a campaign on social media, you will start to see an audience build from an engagement or conversational perspective that lets you know that you're targeting is off. You will want to quickly tighten down your campaign so that you do not continue to spend your budget targeting too wide of an audience.

The intent at this point is not to drive a massive amount of leads, although if this started to happen it would be a good thing in your campaign.

The primary metrics you want to pay attention to in your test phase are your cost per impression, cost per click, cost per cookie, and cost per lead. These are the tangible metrics that you can evaluate based on the strategies we outlined earlier in this book.

Some of the intangibles are the quality of the leads that you're generating or the quality of the audience that you're engaging with.

In this cycle, plan to spend 10% of your budget. Space that out over a 30-day period so that you can determine how much money you can spend each day.

## Optimize Cycle

Once you've completed your test cycle, you will be ready to move into the Optimize cycle. In the Test cycle, we were looking to perfect our ideal buyer targeting to make sure that we have a scalable traffic source to run our campaign through. In this cycle, we're going to assume that we have perfected that traffic source and we're now going to start optimizing the internal elements of our campaign. This could be our ad copy, our landing page, our auto responders, our email sequences, or any element of our end content.

In the next chapter, we're going to show you how to analyze each stage of your campaign to create strategies and improvement. In this cycle, it's a good idea to start A/B testing different elements of your content. Below are some of the most common elements we have found that can be adjusted to improve overall performance of the campaign. This is not a complete list, but a short list of some of the most impactful elements.

**Call to Action (CTA)**: In a campaign that is generating sufficient traffic but not sufficient leads, it's a good idea to look at what your initial call to action is. This can be as simple as changing the button from 'click here' to 'start trial'. Check to make sure that your call to action is direct and leads to a tangible outcome to your visitor.

**Forms**: Forms tend to play a big part in the overall conversion rate of your campaign. We often run into issues where clients have long forms that ask detailed questions at the initial stage of the conversation. Simplifying this to five powerful but simple questions to ask can often increase lead flow and will not decrease value.

**Offer**: Take a look at your overall offer. We often see individuals offering initial consultations or strategy sessions to a cold audience. An audience that does not know you and does not trust you is most likely not looking to talk to you directly already. Even if they do take you up on the offer, your ability to convert someone from cold traffic without learning about their business is very low. Making a tangible offer to the visitor gives them something of value in advance of you talking to them. This often means you need to split test content offers and different conversion paths to bring people into your sales funnel.

**First Point of Reengagement**: This point of reengagement typically can be an auto responder or thank you page that invites the visitor to engage with you further. It's a good idea to split test different offers at this point in order to ensure that the individual continues to move through your sales funnel. Never assume that people are going to continue to move forward on their own. You need to be able to motivate them and entice them to continue to engage with you.

**Next Step**: If all of the elements above are working, you're generating a significant amount of leads, the leads coming through are qualified, and you're getting into the sales conversation, but that is the point where your campaign starts to fall apart, you may want to look at optimizing the next step. The next step is what happens after someone engages with your initial offer. This could be your consultation or strategy session, or could be a push towards engagement with more content. This is often a space where the pass off between marketing and sales fails. If you examine the conversion rate between these two points using the metrics that have been outlined previously in this book, you'll be able to understand where the problem is coming from and how to adjust.

You should spend 20% to 30% of your overall budget in the Optimize cycle. This means you will at least double the amount of budget that you spend from the Test phase to show that you perfected your targeting as well as your conversion paths.

Once you have optimized all of your metrics and your campaign elements, it's time to move into the Convert phase. This is the phase we are going to try to drive maximum ROI.

## Convert Cycle

In the convert phase, you have to be confident that your funnel is in place, that you're targeting is in place, and that you're not willing to scale your traffic. This is where you aggressively begin to spend your budget while maintaining the elements that you previously optimized. Everything from this point forward should be about concentrating on your sales funnel and converting through the pain customers. You should be confident enough in your marketing to let it run and just spend your time working to convert your leads into paying customers.

The biggest mistake marketers make at this point is trying to continue to optimize the campaign from targeting all the way through the conversion. If you have moved into the Conversion phase, you must trust your targeting and your initial offer enough to concentrate on the end of your sales funnel and converting sales-qualified leads into opportunities and into overall wins.

It takes a strong level of confidence and commitment to let the top of your funnel run while you continue to spend your time optimizing for conversion to paying customer. The true reward in doing this is perfecting every element of your campaign from the Test phase to the Optimize phase to the Convert phase, which will ultimately lead to maximum campaign ROI.

This chapter was designed to lay out the strategy and now we will move into the analyze chapter to look at the individual metrics and how to tell what action to take based on what the statistical data tells us.

# SECTION 6:
# TEST & LEARN

CHAPTER 13

# Analyzing Sales and Marketing Efforts

This chapter is designed to give you key indicators of under performance as well as over performance. It may sound strange to be examining for over performance in any of your key metrics, but understanding why this better-than-expected result is happening can give you leverage points to scale your campaign and create greater ROI for your customer or for your business.

We will examine a few marketing metrics as well as a few sales metrics to look for opportunities to improve your overall campaign.

# How to Review Your Primary Metrics

## Target Cost per Lead

### Underperform

If your target cost per lead is well above your budget goal, there are a couple different things that you can look at.

The first is your audience targeting. Misalignment in targeting can lead to a much higher cost per lead than expected. Try to narrow down your focus until you hit your target cost per lead.

If you believe that your targeting is in proper alignment, another cause of a higher-than-expected cost per lead can be your ad copy. Try split testing new images, new calls to action, and new value propositions in your ad copy to try to improve your cost per lead

### Outperform

Having a better-than-expected cost per lead can be both a blessing and a curse. It's important for you to examine the quality of the leads that you're getting to make sure that you're not generating leads in volume at a low cost basis that have no opportunity for future conversion.

In a best-case scenario, you're generating countless high quality leads that are generating potential sales conversations and sales opportunities. If this is the case, this is a leveraging point in your campaign.

### Things to Watch Out For

Your cost per lead can be a distracting indicator. I've had campaigns where the cost per lead was well above our target, yet we were closing sales well below our target cost per sale. I typically ignore the cost per lead and focus on the next metric which is cost per sale. If that number begins to underperform, I will work my way backwards to my cost per lead elements.

## Target cost per sale

### Underperform

This is a critical issue no matter what your budget size is. If the cost per sale is higher than you budgeted, you'll want to start with a top-down analysis of every element of your campaign. Typically with a quick review, you'll find a metric earlier in the funnel that is out of alignment. When you find it, work to fix it.

*Example:*
*We have a target cost per sale of $2,000. We are in the convert phase of our campaign. We closed two sales, but we spent $15,000 to close those sales. This gives us a cost per sale of $7,500 which is well above our target.*

The first thing I would do in this scenario is to look at your Opportunity stage to see how many additional leads you have pending close. Before you jump in and adjust campaign elements, look to close leads that are at the finish line. If you look in this stage and you have a half dozen leads and an expected close rate of 50%, that would give you three additional sales.

*Back to the example:*

*I now have three additional sales to include plus the two I already have = five total sales. From my $15,000 spend, five sales = $3,000 per sale. This is still above my target, but much better than $7,500 per sale.*

If you go back to your Opportunity stage and you do not have any additional opportunities to close, then you need to work down your sales stages one at a time looking for the issue. Where in the cycle did things start to fall apart? We'll cover each stage in this chapter.

## Outperform

It seems counterintuitive to document what to do when your cost per sale is below your target. When this happens, you have a scaling opportunity. If you have the capacity to handle more clients, it's time to max out those credit cards. This doesn't happen often, so when it does take advantage of it and look to grow your business or your client's business as much as possible. The worst thing you can do is stick to the current budget. You'll miss a great opportunity that doesn't come around all that often.

## Things to Watch Out For

Don't get caught up measuring this too early in the campaign. When you make your first sale, you'll always be off target. It's about momentum and understanding your metrics as the campaign progresses.

# Target ROI

You should be starting to see that all of these metrics relate to one another. If your cost per sale is inline, then your target ROI should be inline as well. If you're closing customers at your target price point, that is.

### Underperform

At this point, look to make sure you're on budget with your spend. If you're working with an agency, make sure they didn't get ahead of the weekly spend that was outlined. Walk through each of your funnel metrics to see where the drop off may be occurring and adjust accordingly.

### Outperform

Just as with target cost per sale, if you're outperforming your goals from an ROI point of view, then look to increase spend. Attack opportunities when they come up.

### Things to Watch Out For

If all other elements are inline but you're still not reaching your target ROI, look at the discounts you may have offered. Often they can derail a great campaign when they are not preplanned.

# Prospect to Marketing Qualified Lead (MQL)

Converting a prospect to an MQL is an act of marketing. If you're not reaching your target conversion rate, it's time to sit down with the marketing team.

### Underperform

Look at your initial engagement point. If you're doing email marketing, start with the subject line of your email. If you're getting opens but not responses or click-throughs, then adjust your copy. This all comes down to that initial touch point. It's the first element of your marketing that a lead interacts with. You'll want to spend a lot of time getting this right.

### Outperform

If you're getting a much higher percentage of prospects engaging with your marketing, then move on to the next stage. It's great when this happens. Don't worry about scaling this stage until you've reached campaign ROI and have all of your metrics in the outperform stage.

### Things to Watch Out For

This is the first thing that can break in your campaign. If you don't put the time and resources into getting this stage right, you'll never reach the next stage. This will cause your entire campaign to break down. Once you've hit your target conversion rate, you'll want to move on quickly. The money comes later in the funnel so don't get obsessed with this stage. Get it to the goal and then move on.

## MQL to SQL

The larger the organization, the more likely you are to have issues at this stage. This is the point where marketing has qualified the lead and engaged the lead. It's now time to hand the lead off to sales. Getting this process right is critical to generating revenue.

## Underperform

If you're underperforming at this stage, I would look at the three following things:

**Process**: What is your documented hand off process? Simply sending a lead notification to Sales isn't enough. It is typically better to have Marketing hand deliver a qualified and engaged lead to Sales so there can be a full review of the lead's data. This will ensure a proper handoff.

**Technology**: Every CRM has a different method of converting a lead to the Sales stage. Documenting your technology process and reviewing it on an ongoing basis will ensure that all team members know how to use it and that they use it correctly.

**Acceptance**: If your marketing team hasn't done a good job of properly qualifying leads in the past, your sales team may not be willing to accept new leads. This can cause a major breakdown in your campaign. We see this a lot in companies that have haphazardly implemented data-driven marketing in their business. A lead must be fully qualified and fully engaged to move to SQL.

## Outperform

If your Process, Technology, and Acceptance are in order, you should have no problem outperforming your goals. There are, however, a few things to look out for.

**Things to Watch Out For**

The critical breakdown at this stage is passing through unqualified or unengaged leads. This can cause the metric to look good while creating a disconnect between Sales and Marketing that can be catastrophic in the next stage.

# SQL to Opportunity

They're qualified, they're engaged, and they're interested – seems like a home run to me. But what can happen at this stage to stop the proposal process?

**Underperform**

If Sales is getting a good amount of Sales Qualified Leads from Marketing but struggling to move those leads to the Opportunity stage, there is usually an issue with marketing efforts. You'll want to review your persona targeting to make sure there is alignment from a data perspective. You'll then want to review the hand off process. If everything looks good with those, then you'll have to consider the offer.

This book was designed to help bring a proven offer to market through data-driven marketing. This improves efficiencies and scalability. If you get to this point and you're offer isn't converting, you'll want to go back to each of the lost leads to ask them what is it about our offer that caused you to not move forward.

Here are a few things we tend to see:
- **Price**: Are you competitively priced?
- **Understanding**: Do we believe you understand our problem well enough to help us?

- **Solution**: Do we believe your solution will solve our problem?
- **Credibility**: Do we believe you're a credible provider of the solution you offer?
- **Sales** Process: Is your sales process easy to navigate?
- **Presentation**: Did you present your offer in a manner that is engaging?

These elements go beyond data-driven marketing and move into the world of salesmanship. I have a few books to recommend if you're struggling at this point:

www.TheDataDrivenMarketer.com/Sales

The list is always changing as I read new books.

## Outperform

If your sales team is getting qualified and properly engaged leads, you should have no issue at this stage.

## Things to Watch Out For

This can be a false indicator as well. If your conversion metric is high here but you're not getting wins, you'll want to check to make sure your sales team isn't just sending out proposals blindly. We've seen this happen. A proper proposal process includes a review phone call to make sure that both parties are satisfied with the details of the agreement. Without that completed call, you can't count emailing them an agreement as a conversion to opportunity.

# Opportunity to Win

Where are all my bell ringers? This is the critical stage. You've spent time and resources to bring a data-driven marketing campaign to live. You've worked your sales stages and moved your lead successfully to the point of close. What could go wrong?

## Underperform

If you're seeing a decent conversion rate of SQL to Opportunity but you're not closing deals, you'll want to review your closing process. What we tend to see here is a lack of a process to move a lead to close. This includes not setting a kickoff date in the proposal process. You do not want to deliver a proposal to someone without a timeframe on it. This can be a time-sensitive offer, or it could be an implementation queue that they want to get into. Don't let the buyer control the close date. If you do, they can drag this out as far as they want.

## Outperform

If you're closing more deals than you had planned while maintaining your price, then keep doing it. This is the best problem you could have.

## Things to Watch Out For

Don't let your team celebrate a win until payment has been processed. It seems off that I would need to say this, but I've seen it happen too often. You'll get a commitment on an agreement and the team will start to celebrate. We don't exist in a vacuum. There is often a competitor on the other end looking to undercut you any way they can. Keep pressing the deal until you have a check or have processed a credit card.

# CHAPTER 14

# Refine

What do you do after the campaign has been completed? The first thing to understand is that unless you sell your company, you are never done marketing. From the day you start your business until the day that it's sold, marketing will be a primary driver of your overall business success. In the businesses that I have seen fail, it's never because they ran out of money; it's just because they didn't invest enough in marketing early in the business.

What are some of the strategies that you can implement in order to refine and prepare for your next campaign?

## Review Your Metrics

A substantial amount of this book was spent defining what the primary metrics of a data-driven marketing campaign are, how to use them to target your ideal buyer, how to leverage those metrics to launch a successful campaign, and then how to analyze those metrics to make sure that your campaign is performing on par with your goals. When the campaign is done, it's time to reevaluate every metric that you have laid out to review them for opportunities for improvement in your next campaign.

## Review Your CRM

You want to do a deep dive in to every lead that has made it into the Marketing Qualified Lead or better sales cycle stage. Each lead that has been engaged at this point is an opportunity to generate revenue. Look for opportunities where leads may have stalled or may have been overlooked. Make sure that all of your data for each of your leads is completely up to date. Also, look for opportunities to segment out leads based on what you've learned from your first campaign. There may be opportunities to target a subset of your ideal buyer in order to generate revenue from an upsell or cross sell of your current product or promotion.

## Adjust Your Audience Platform

In previous chapters, we talked about the different platforms you can use to engage your audience. What did you learn in your first campaign that would tell you that your current platform is correct or if you should make adjustments? This is a great time to test additional platforms or to build a cross platform strategy that allows you to connect with a larger audience to grow your ability to sell.

Take everything that you learned and all of the statistical data that you analyzed and begin to outline a new goal for a new campaign. Campaign development in data-driven marketing is progressive. This means that once one campaign completes, the next one should already be built and ready to start. The more time you spend perfecting your data-driven marketing skills, the easier it will be for you to roll out new campaigns in the future and even have multiple campaigns running across different audience platforms or making different initial offers.

The Refinement stage is a great opportunity to document as a case study what you've learned in your own campaigns in as well as the campaigns that you've done for clients. It's this education and this analysis that helps you to become a top data-driven marketer.

# CHAPTER 15

# Data Hygiene

Clean and correct data is the key to achieving the best results from your database, so let's break down what we need to keep an eye on.

Your campaign is only as good as your data. Despite the fact that smart marketers know data is the bread and butter of their campaigns, few take the time to 'clean' their contact lists and marketing metrics. According to Ascend2, 35% of marketers know they have dirty data and only 8% intend to do something about it.

This means a large chunk of the marketing campaigns currently deployed are built on *educated guesses* instead of data. What's the point of investing into a data-driven marketing strategy if you're not going to maintain your database and polish your data?

Don't make the mistake of thinking that your database will maintain itself. You need to regularly clean your data and take active measures to implement 'hygienic' data practices in your campaigns. For example, to keep your lead lists up to date, implement a rule that whoever touches the account must make note of that in the comment sections.

## 5 Ways Dirty Data Affects Your Marketing Campaigns

Your database isn't going to maintain itself. Failing to keep your data clean can result in a lot of problems throughout your data-driven marketing strategy.

### 1. Poor quality data can have a huge impact on your email marketing open rates.

If you're sending emails to dead email addresses, you can bet no one's going to open them. ISPs measure your deliverability and open rates. Continuing to send emails to bad email addresses kills your email performance.

**2. Sales suffer.**

Have you ever been called by a salesperson who was asking for a person that doesn't work at your company? It's pretty annoying, right? When you're not keeping contacts up to date, your sales performance suffers.

**3. Your KPIs are impacted by bad data.**

From email marketing scores to click through rates and sales performance, poor quality data impacts every facet of your data-driven marketing campaign.

**4. You start trying to sell to the wrong customers.**

If you're building your persona assumptions based on the data in your CRM that is out of date, you could be creating entire campaigns that target the wrong potential buyers.

**5. Marketing becomes a black hole in your budget.**

When organizations complain about poor open rates and conversion rates, the root cause is usually bad data. Bad data in equals bad results out. It takes work, but bad data will tax your marketing budget and destroy your sales potential. Who wants to pick up a second phone call from someone who got their name wrong? No one.

## 5-Step Data Cleansing Process

To cleanse your data, go through a systematic process that allows you to first evaluate what needs to be done and then guides you through an implementation process to do it correctly and efficiently.

## 1. Audit Your Data

The first step in this process is to audit your data. This is a visual evaluation you go through from your sales funnel down to the individual contact data looking to evaluate your list and to document potential problems that we will solve in later steps.

When looking at this from a top-down perspective, one of the primary KPIs that we like to look at is data accuracy scores. This is typically done at each level of the sales funnel where you're looking for progressively better data accuracy scores as contacts move through the sales process. This allows you to identify data needs in each of your sales funnel stages so that problems can be addressed in bulk.

Once you've completed your audit and outlined some of the macro issues that you face from a data accuracy perspective, it's a good idea to manually correct the things that you see are easily correctable.

## 2. Correct What You Can

This can be moving contacts into the correct stage of a sales funnel or removing contacts from sales funnel stages that you know have fallen off. Also, take advantage of this time to reach back out to contacts that may have been missed in previous efforts.

In later stages, we're going to use technology to help improve our overall data quality. However, that technology will not know where your contacts are in your sales funnel so it's important when you do your hygiene reviews to update this data to be as accurate as possible.

## 3. Combine Data

The next stage is to combine records. If you've done everything absolutely perfectly up to this point you probably will not have any records that need to be combined. Let's be honest with ourselves, no one ever implemented this perfectly.

There are two types of record combinations we typically face inside organizations.

The first is combining data that has been spread out across multiple tools or even piles of business cards and sticky notes that were never entered into their CRM. It is better for you to understand that this happens so that you have a process for capturing this data than it is to believe that everyone on your sales team or your client's sales team is going to use the technology correctly each time.

The second is to combine individual contact records in the company records. Over time, you may speak with different individuals from the same company. That can lead to problems if you're not combining efforts and understanding who you are speaking to in an organization. When you combine contact records, you can set the priority and the decision-maker while still keeping in contact with subordinates who can help you to convert the sale.

Now that we've done the manual part, it's time to bring in some technology partners in order to help us improve the overall data hygiene of our list.

## 4. Cleanse Your Data

The first thing that we're going to do is cleanse our list. The data providers that were mentioned in the technology section can help you to do this quickly and efficiently. A cleanse is primarily done to make sure that the email address and contact record data that we have is still accurate and usable. As no one stays with the same company for more than a few years in today's ever-changing environment, it's important to know when an email address is no longer good. The quarterly or annual cleanse of your list will help you to ensure that you maintain high-quality email statistics with ISPs.

It will also help you to ensure that you're not dedicating sales and marketing resources to individuals that are no longer with a company.

## 5. Enrich Your Data

The last step in proper data hygiene is to enrich your data. As we implement data-driven marketing campaigns, we're going to be adding new contacts to our database. As those contacts are added, we may not have all of the critical data about that organization or individual that is available. The data providers mentioned in the technology section can help you enrich your list to capture data points about the organization or the job title of the contacts that you added to your database.

This really is a rinse and repeat process. High-achieving organizations typically run this process on a quarterly basis. At the very least, you should run this on an annual basis or at the onset of investment in a new data-driven marketing campaign.

If you were a digital marketing agency who's taking on new clients, we are going to run a data-driven marketing campaign for them. This is a value-added service their organizations will pay a good amount of money for and that will also help you leverage success when you move to implementation.

# Closing

This book was designed to give you a tactical roadmap to implementing a data driven marketing campaign.

The story doesn't end here. To get more free resources and to connect with our team about your data-driven marketing efforts, head over to www.enfusen.com

Good luck!

– Roger Bryan

If you like what you've read in this book head on over to https://www.enfusen.com and sign up for a trial. You can use the code "DataDriven50" to receive a LIFETIME Discount of 50% off any subscription.

# Downloadable Content Offers for Your Data-Driven Strategy

Download the full data-driven checklist here:

https://www.enfusen.com/data-driven-marketing-checklist/

Follow the exclusive data-driven marketing Facebook page here: Facebook.com/MarketingWithRoger

# SECTION 7:
# RESOURCES

# 12-Step Quick Start Checklist

**Step 1:** What are the overall goals of your data-driven campaign?

_____

_____

_____

_____

_____

**Step 2:** What data do you need acquire to start your campaign?

_____

_____

_____

_____

_____

**Step 3:** Where can you get the data you need?

_____

_____

_____

_____

_____

**Step 4:** Define your ideal buyer (five primary data points?)

_____

_____

_____

_____

_____

**Step 5:** What content will you need to create for your campaign?

_____

_____

_____

_____

_____

**Step 6:** What marketing channel will you choose?

_____

_____

_____

_____

_____

**Step 7:** What technology will you need for your campaign?

_____

_____

_____

_____

_____

**Step 8:** Outline your team and what each will do in this process.

_____

_____

_____

_____

_____

**Step 9:** What is your offer?

_____

_____

_____

_____

_____

**Step 10:** What are your expected conversion rates at each stage of your campaign?

_____

_____

_____

_____

_____

**Step 11:** What is the expected campaign completion date?

_____

_____

_____

_____

_____

**Step 12:** How will you document your campaign progress for review?

_____

_____

_____

_____

_____

# Glossary of Terms

**Campaigns** – Work in an organized and active way toward a particular goal, typically towards a specific offer or marketing goal.

**Content** – Any copy, graphics, or consumable media that nurtures visitors to your brand or organization.

**Content Insight Engine** – A tool that uses content analytics to predict the outcome of content campaigns.

**Content Marketing** – A strategic marketing style that focuses on sharing relevant and consistent content to your buyer personas

**Content Marketing Analytics** – Collective data built off prearranged metrics about the content you post put into spreadsheets.

**Content Recommendation Engine** – An engine designed to recommend content that has performed well and shows promise on continuing its performance.

**Cost Per Click** – The price tag attached to paid-for traffic determined by keyword traffic and cost that is managed through SEM and PPC.

**Cost Per Lead** – Online advertising pricing model that involves an offer between the advertiser and the consumer through the sharing of information.

**Cost Per View** – This is similar to CPC, but is the dollar amount attached to a video interaction or advertisement.

**Customer Relationship Manager (CRM)** – The practices, strategies and technologies that are used to manage and analyze customer interactions and data through your sales cycle. These systems collect data on customers according to sign-up information and interaction.

**CRM Insight Engine** – A system that recommends content for different leads based on preset actions, qualifications, and interactions.

**Customer Data** – The collection of data that represents how customers interact with your marketing offers and organization as a whole.

**Customer Lifetime Value** – A simple equation that factors different parts of customer-value metrics that come to average outcomes of expected customer value over a period of time.

**Customer Persona** – The demographics, statistics, and marketing data that tell you who your ideal customer is and how your product or service needs to appeal to those needs.

**Customer Value** – Customer value splits into two categories, and references the feeling of a customer about the product or service before and after purchase. Desired Value is what customers are looking for before they buy, and Perceived Value is how the customer feels about the product or services after purchasing.

**Data-Driven Marketing** – The act of leveraging customer data to create intelligent campaigns with predictable and dependable growth.

**Data Science** – The process of extracting data and organizing it in order to conduct in-depth analysis.

**Data-Wrangling** – The process of connecting different sets of data to organize over all results and consistent consumption.

**Demographics** – Information about your market that tells you who your customers are and what their interests are.

**Digital Marketing** – The marketing of products or services using digital technologies. Through the Internet, you can connect through mobile devices and computers by displaying advertising and other digital content.

**Engagement Data** – The marketing data that represents how leads and customers interact with your different marketing channels (for example, opening emails, interacting on social media, etc.)

**Email Marketing** – Outreach through email to individuals who have given their information.

**Email Marketing Insight Engine** – A recommended engine for email marketing that helps you promote email interactions that perform well, and allows you the ability to see and revamp ones that are not performing well.

**Inbound links** – Links from other websites that lead to a page on your site.

**Inbound Marketing** – The use of blogs, podcasts, video, eBooks, newsletters, whitepapers, SEP, physical products, social media, and other content platforms to nurture customer through the different stages of the sales cycle.

**Inbound Marketing Analytics** – Data generated from your customers' interactions with your content.

**Insight Engines** – Engines on a Marketing Cloud that provide suggestions on strategy and content by analyzing current and historical marketing data.

**Key Performance Indicators (KPI)** – A KPI is a measurable value that demonstrates how effectively a company is achieving sales and marketing goals.

**Keyword Insight Engine** – A tool designed to help you choose keywords based on competition, reach, and cost.

**Landing Page** – The section of a website accessed by clicking a hyperlink on another web page, typically the website's home page.

**Lead Scoring** – The act of attaching a value, stage, and contact history to a sales or marketing qualified prospect.

**Lead Stages** – The stages that a potential customer goes through to become an active customer.

**Marketing Activities** – Any effort you make to reach potential or current customers that has been planned by your sales and marketing teams.

**Marketing Automation** – Software platforms and technologies designed for marketing that automate repetitive tasks.

**Marketing Data** – Collection of data used to make marketing decisions based on metrics set by the company.

**Marketing Funnel** – The detailed process and operations of a journey your customer takes to become an active buyer.

**Marketing Productivity** – The level of success incurred from marketing activities in an established period of time.

**Marketing Control Center** (MCC) – Administrative operational center from Enfusen that supplies powerful analytics, planning, and predictive recommendation.

**Metrics** – A method of measuring something, or the results obtained from this.

**Organic Traffic** – Visitors that interact with your website and business online that did not find your company through a paid web traffic source.

**Outbound Links** – Links your brand to credible sources and creates doorways of credibility within the industry.

**Predictive Analytics** – Predictive analytics represents a variety of software and programs that use predictive models to show consumer reaction, consumption, and make inferences on future campaigns.

**Return on Investment (ROI)** – Metric that details how much revenue each of your investments made for the business.

To calculate ROI, the benefit (return) of an investment is divided by the cost of the investment; the result is expressed as a percentage, or a ratio.

**Sales Automation** – Automates business sales tasks such as inventory control, sales processing, and tracking of customer interactions, and analyzes sales performance.

**Sales cycle** – Series of predictable phases required to sell your product or service to the market.

**Search Engine Optimization** – Process of maximizing the number of visitors to a particular website by ensuring that the site appears high on the list of results returned by a search engine.

**SEM Campaign** – Paid traffic campaigns that are meant to forward leads to a landing page or interactive offer.

**Site Audit Insight Engine** – A system designed to audit your site and give you recommendations on what needs to be changed.

**Telesales** – Selling of goods or services over the telephone.

**Virtual CMO** – A Chief Marketing Officer from a stand-alone location there to work with your brand to help you succeed.

# Blogs and Websites

Author, Guest. "WordStream." *5 Killer Examples of Data-Driven Marketing.* WordStream, 29 Aug. 2016. Web. 29 Sept. 2016.

    www.wordstream.com/blog/ws/2016/08/25/data-driven-marketing

    www.google.com/#safe=off&q=data+driven+marketing

Edelman, By David C. "Four Ways to Get More Value from Digital Marketing." *McKinsey & Company.* McKinsey & Company, Mar. 2010. Web. 29 Sept. 2016.

    http://www.mckinsey.com/business-functions/marketing-and-sales/our-insights/four-ways-to-get-more-value-from-digital-marketing

    http://blog.knowtify.io/33-best-quotes-on-customer-engagement/

Juba, Mike. "Online Marketing Strategies to Increase Online Revenue." *Business 2 Community Comments.* B2C, 16 June 2014. Web. 29 Sept. 2016.

    http://www.business2community.com/online-marketing/online-marketing-strategies-increase-online-revenue-0914156

Upfront Analytics Team, The. "What Are the Benefits of Using Databases to Analyze Marketing Research Data?" Analytics Upfront, 19 Nov. 2015. Web. 29 Sept. 2016.

http://upfrontanalytics.com/what-are-the-benefits-of-using-databases-to-analyze-marketing-research-data/

*How to Set Marketing Goals Based on Business Goals.*
IMPACT, 11 May 2016. Web. 29 Sept. 2016.
https://www.impactbnd.com/blog/how-to-set-marketing-goals-based-on-business-goals

Jay Conrad Levinson and Al Lautenslager. "This Is How You Come Up With Marketing Goals." *Entrepreneur.*
Entrepreneur, 3 June 2014. Web. 29 Sept. 2016.
https://www.entrepreneur.com/article/234204

@wholebrainprez. "16 Tips for Developing Your 2016 Sales and Marketing Strategy." *16 Tips for Developing Your 2016 Sales and Marketing Strategy.* The Whole Brain Group, 21 Jan. 2016. Web. 29 Sept. 2016.
http://blog.thewholebraingroup.com/16-tips-developing-sales-marketing-strategy

Voice, ADP. "How A Data-Driven Employee Review Process Can Help Your Company Develop Talent." *Forbes.*
Forbes Magazine, 1 Feb. 2016. Web. 29 Sept. 2016.
http://www.forbes.com/sites/adp/2016/02/01/how-a-data-driven-employee-review-process-can-help-your-company-develop-talent/

@danielku20. "The Effective Sales Process: A Data Driven Approach [Infographic]." *The Effective Sales Process: A Data Driven Approach [Infographic].* Sales For Life, 4 Dec. 2015.
Web. 29 Sept. 2016.

http://www.salesforlife.com/blog/sales-process-2/the-data-driven-approach-to-creating-an-effective-sales-process-infographic/

Group, Grow VC. "The Transition Towards a More Data-driven Investment Process in the Private Market." *Enabling Digital Finance*. Grow VC Group, 19 Oct. 2015. Web. 29 Sept. 2016.
http://www.growvc.com/blog/2015/10/the-transition-towards-a-more-data-driven-investment-process-in-the-private-market/

Solution, By. "Creating A Data-Driven Sales Process." *Creating A Data-Driven Sales Process*. Datanyze, 4 May 2016. Web. 29 Sept. 2016.
https://resources.datanyze.com/h/i/257282916-creating-a-data-driven-sales-process

Enfusen. "Enfusen - Data Driven Marketing Software for Smart Marketers." *Enfusen*. Enfusen, n.d. Web. 29 Sept. 2016.
https://www.enfusen.com/

SharpSpring. "Simple, Easy, Affordable Marketing Automation | SharpSpring." *SharpSpring*. SharpSpring, n.d. Web. 29 Sept. 2016.
https://sharpspring.com/

Weber, Alan. "14 No-Fail Steps to Building a Database." *TargetMarketing*. TargetMarketing, 1 Oct. 2000. Web. 29 Sept. 2016.

http://www.targetmarketingmag.com/article/14-no-fail-steps-building-database-28255/all/

Kaminsky, Robert. "How Much Is Enough? A Basic Guide to Market Research Section Purchasing." *How Much Is Enough? A Basic Guide to Market Research Section Purchasing*. MarketResearch.com, 25 May 2015. Web. 29 Sept. 2016.
http://blog.marketresearch.com/how-much-is-enough-a-basic-guide-to-market-research-section-purchasing

Bonnell, Ashlan. "Top 10 FAQs When Purchasing Market Research." *Top 10 FAQs When Purchasing Market Research*. MarketResearch.com, 8 May 2014. Web. 29 Sept. 2016.
http://blog.marketresearch.com/top-10-faqs-when-purchasing-market-research

Cleanthous, Alex. "14 List Building Hacks to Grow Your Email Database Fast." *ConversionXL*. ConversionXL, 05 Nov. 2015. Web. 29 Sept. 2016.
http://conversionxl.com/14-list-building-hacks-grow-email-database-fast/

@MarcHerschberge. "4 Strategies to Help Maintain Lead Quality in Your Database." *4 Strategies to Help Maintain Lead Quality in Your Database*. HubSpot, 25 Nov. 2015. Web. 29 Sept. 2016.
http://blog.hubspot.com/marketing/maintain-database-lead-quality

@ekwking. "6 Quick Tips to Improve Lead Database Quality." *Marketo Marketing Blog Best Practices and Thought Leadership*. Marketo, 08 Oct. 2015. Web. 29 Sept. 2016.
http://blog.marketo.com/2015/10/6-quick-ways-to-improve-lead-database-quality.html

@Exchangeleads. "The High Cost of Bad Data – Building Your Marketing Database." *Exchange Leads*. Exchange Leads, 17 Nov. 2015. Web. 29 Sept. 2016.
http://exchangeleads.io/the-high-cost-of-bad-data-building-your-marketing-database/

Forrestal Consultants LLC. "Purchasing Research." *Forrestal Consultants LLC*. Forrestal Consultants LLC, n.d. Web. 29 Sept. 2016.
http://www.forrestalconsultants.com/purchasing-research/

@SelineOK. "Tips for Buying Market Research Reports." *Tips for Buying Market Research Reports*. MarketResearch.com, 23 Oct. 2015. Web. 29 Sept. 2016.
http://blog.marketresearch.com/tips-for-buying-market-research-reports

By Combining Informa and FastStats, Brands Have Comprehensive Control of Their Customer Database and How the Data Is Presented and Used across the Organisation. "Putting Data On The Menu - Integrated Multi-Channel Marketing Services | Multi Award Winners." *Integrated Multi-Channel Marketing Services*. Alchemetrics, 23 Feb. 2016. Web. 29 Sept. 2016.
http://home.alchemetrics.co.uk/putting-data-on-the-menu/

VisualIQ. "Disparate Data and Devices." *Integrating Your Disparate Marketing Data*. VisualIQ, n.d. Web. 29 Sept. 2016.
http://www.visualiq.com/challenges/integrated-marketing-data

@Gareth_giggs. "How to Integrate Your Data and Achieve a Marketing Operations Peace of Mind." *Marketo Marketing Blog Best Practices and Thought Leadership*. Marketo, 25 May 2016. Web. 29 Sept. 2016.
http://blog.marketo.com/2016/03/how-to-integrate-your-data-and-achieve-a-marketing-operations-peace-of-mind.html

@ballantinecorp. "Crash Course Guide on Data Hygiene - Ballantine." *Ballantine*. Ballantine, 18 June 2015. Web. 29 Sept. 2016.
https://www.ballantine.com/crash-course-guide-on-data-hygiene/

Rouse, Margaret. "What Is Data Hygiene? - Definition from WhatIs.com." *WhatIs.com*. WhatIs.com, Apr. 2013. Web. 29 Sept. 2016.
http://whatis.techtarget.com/definition/data-hygiene

@Exchangeleads. "The High Cost of Bad Data – Building Your Marketing Database." *Exchange Leads*. Exchange Leads, 17 Nov. 2015. Web. 29 Sept. 2016.
http://exchangeleads.io/the-high-cost-of-bad-data-building-your-marketing-database

@CMIContent. "Buyer Personas That Build Sales." *Content Marketing Institute*. Content Marketing Institue, 13 July 2016. Web. 29 Sept. 2016.

http://contentmarketinginstitute.com/2016/05/build-buyer-personas/

@lkolow. "20 Questions to Ask When Creating Buyer Personas [Free Template]." *20 Questions to Ask When Creating Buyer Personas [Free Template]*. HubSpot, 6 Oct. 2015. Web. 29 Sept. 2016.

http://blog.hubspot.com/blog/tabid/6307/bid/30907/9-Questions-You-Need-to-Ask-When-Developing-Buyer-Personas.aspx

@pamelump. "How to Create Detailed Buyer Personas for Your Business [Free Persona Template]." *How to Create Detailed Buyer Personas for Your Business [Free Persona Template]*. HubSpot, 28 May 2015. Web. 29 Sept. 2016.

http://blog.hubspot.com/blog/tabid/6307/bid/33491/Everyt hing-Marketers-Need-to-Research-Create-Detailed-Buyer-Personas-Template.aspx

Team, Writtent. "How to Build an Epic Buyer Persona Profile | Writtent." *Writtent*. Writtent, 04 Aug. 2016. Web. 29 Sept. 2016.

http://writtent.com/blog/building-an-epic-buyer-persona-profile-a-totally-comprehensive-guide/

Hines, Kristi. "How to Use Facebook Audience Insights to Unlock Buyer Personas." *Salesforce Canada Blog*. SalesForce, 25 Jan. 2016. Web. 29 Sept. 2016.

https://www.salesforce.com/ca/blog/2016/01/facebook-buyer-personas.html

@CMIContent. "The 3 Biggest Mistakes Marketers Make With Buyer Personas (2016 Edition)." *Content Marketing Institute*. Content Marketing Institue, 26 Aug. 2016. Web. 29 Sept. 2016.
http://contentmarketinginstitute.com/2016/08/mistakes-buyer-personas/

@BobMusial. "How to Define Your Sales Process Stages." *How to Define Your Sales Process Stages*. HubSpot, 14 Jan. 2016. Web. 29 Sept. 2016.
http://blog.hubspot.com/sales/how-to-define-your-sales-process-stages

HubSpot. "Creating a Sales Process: The Ultimate Guide | HubSpot." *Creating a Sales Process: The Ultimate Guide | HubSpot*. HubSpot, n.d. Web. 29 Sept. 2016.
http://www.hubspot.com/sales/sales-process

Investopedia, Root. "Brand Awareness." *Investopedia*. Investopedia, 24 May 2006. Web. 09 Jan. 2017.

@CMIContent. "6 Steps to a Data-Driven Content Marketing Strategy." *Content Marketing Institute*. Content Marketing Institue, 05 Aug. 2014. Web. 29 Sept. 2016.
http://contentmarketinginstitute.com/2014/06/data-driven-content-marketing-strategy/

@CMIContent. "Data-Driven Content Strategy Meets Content Marketing [Essential Template]." *Content Marketing Institute*. Content Marketing Institute, 24 June 2016. Web. 29 Sept. 2016.
http://contentmarketinginstitute.com/2015/09/data-driven-content-strategy-template/

@courtneyseiter. "20 Great Social Media Voices (And How To Develop Your Own)." *Marketing Land*. Marketing Land, 21 Aug. 2012. Web. 29 Sept. 2016.
http://marketingland.com/20-great-social-media-voices-and-how-to-develop-your-own-18057

Linn, @michelelinn. "Developing a Content Strategy." *Content Marketing Institute*. Content Marketing Institute, n.d. Web. 29 Sept. 2016.

*Forbes*. Forbes Magazine, 3 Jan. 2016. Web. 29 Sep. 2016.
http://www.forbes.com/sites/sujanpatel/2016/01/03/what-your-2016-content-marketing-strategy-should-look-like/

@Corey_bos. "Content Marketing Strategy: A Comprehensive Guide for Modern Marketers." *Content Marketing Strategy: A Comprehensive Guide for Modern Marketers*. HubSpot, 21 July 2015. Web. 29 Sept. 2016.
http://blog.hubspot.com/marketing/content-marketing-strategy-guide

# Books

Artun, Omer, and Dominique Levin. *Predictive Marketing: Easy Ways Every Marketer Can Use Customer Analytics a.* N.p.: John Wiley & Sons, 2015. Print.

Glass, Russell, and Sean Callahan. *The Big Data-driven Business: How to Use Big Data to Win Customers, Beat Competitors, and Boost Profits.* N.p.: n.p., n.d. Print.

Jeffery, Mark. *Data-driven Marketing: The 15 Metrics Everyone in Marketing Should Know.* Hoboken, NJ: John Wiley, 2010. Print.

Ross, Aaron, and Marylou Tyler. *Predictable Revenue: Turn Your Business into a Sales Machine with the $100 Million Best Practices of Salesforce.com.* West Hollywood, CA: PebbleStorm, 2012. Print.

Stevens, Ruth P., and Theresa A. Kushner. *B2B Data-driven Marketing: Sources, Uses, Results.* N.p.: n.p., n.d. Print.

Semmelroth, David. *Data Marketing for Dummies.* Hoboken, NJ: John Wiley & Sons, 2013. Print.

# Research Papers

@Gartner_Inc. "Build the Right Team for Data-Driven Marketing - Smarter With Gartner." *Smarter With Gartner*. N.p., 03 Oct. 2016. Web. 14 Oct. 2016.
www.gartner.com/smarterwithgartner/build-the-right-team-for-data-driven-marketing/

S.A.S. *Customer Intelligence in the Era of Data-driven Marketing*. Cary, NC: n.p., 2015. PDF.

Gartner. *Agenda Overview for Data-Driven Marketing, 2015*. Stamford, CT: n.p., 29 Dec. 2014. PDF.

74004052R00099

Made in the USA
Middletown, DE
19 May 2018